The Guide to a Dead Brilliant Funeral Speech

Because you only get one chance to make a last impression

Neil Dorward

The Guide to a Dead Brilliant Funeral Speech

First published in 2009 by

Ecademy Press

6, Woodland Rise, Penryn, Cornwall, UK. TR10 8QD

info@ecademy-press.com

www.ecademy-press.com

Printed and Bound by Lightning Source in the UK and USA

Set in Warnock Pro and Meta by Charlotte Mouncey

Printed on acid-free paper from managed forests. This book is printed on demand, so no copies will be remaindered or pulped.

ISBN 978-1-905823-56-7

Acknowledgments and thanks to

Clare, Phil, Kate, Sally, Carole, Paul and Margaret.

Forewords

Dally Messenger III
Principal, International College of Celebrancy

Polonius - What do you read, my lord?
Hamlet - Words, words, words. (Hamlet 2.2)

Human beings mainly communicate through words. And words are important. Words - and how they are spoken – can change the course of history. George Bush Senior won a presidential election in the USA by asking three words "Where's the beef?" Winston Churchill stirred and inspired a nation with his words – "We will fight them on the beaches ..." or his ringing but simple 1940 tribute - "Never in the field of human conflict was so much owed by so many to so few".

John F Kennedy has these words on his tomb – "ask not what your country can do for you - ask what you can do for your country". Perhaps the most famous words which raised awareness and championed the cause of human freedom came from a black clergyman – Martin Luther King Jnr when he dreamed – "I have a dream that my four little children will one day live in a nation where they will not be judged by the color of their skin but by the content of their character."

So words can have great power.

As a Celebrant with at least two thousand funerals behind me, and at least an equal number of conversations and discussions, I can ask you, the reader of this valuable little volume, is there anything that has riled you more than the wrong words said at a funeral? Have you been to a funeral when the deceased's name was pronounced wrongly, or their worthy deeds were not mentioned, or the eulogist got the facts wrong? Didn't you feel sick in the stomach?

Here's the rub – a funeral is a one chance, only chance occasion. If you don't get it right the first time, there is no second chance. That is why the professional qualified Civil Funeral Celebrant, one who is conscientious and responsible, is a very precious and rare being in our society. Neil Dorward is one such.

Let me get one other thing straight, dear reader – and please take it in – there is no such thing as a short cut to a good funeral. No such thing. It takes hours of painstaking research and preparation, a competent Celebrant and professional speaker is worth their weight in gold and Neil Dorward's book will assist the Celebrancy Profession to ensure the highest standards of excellence are met and the right words and stories are delivered in the most meaningful and comforting way.

Pam Vetter – The Funeral Lady (USA)

When I first came into contact with Neil, grateful tears came to my eyes because he understood completely that the funeral service belongs to the family. He willingly exchanges drafts of funerals with the family prior to service. As such, Neil includes the family in every part of the process so there will be no surprises at the funeral, when they are encompassed in grief.

Neil offers steps to help Celebrants that can't be found in any other books. This book is different from every book and is much needed. This information is specifically geared to the funeral and the Celebrant. How will we deal with suicide, murder, or children? Celebrancy is not easy work, but it is amazing work. We have the ability to help a family start healing even after the most devastating loss has occurred.

A funeral is a memorable, poetic wave of farewell to a loved one. Neil Dorward and I agree on this premise wholeheartedly. Every funeral doesn't have to be dressed up in a wealth of famous poems or famous quotes, but the poetry develops through sharing a life story from a family's heart. To capture the poetry of a life, a Celebrant meets with the family, listens to their vision, maps out a planned service, and compiles life stories into honest prose that is captivating, communicates with the family, and effectively shares the importance of a life to an audience of friends and family. While this is a great responsibility, this process is also storytelling at its best. In the end, a Celebrant should fulfil a family's vision of a meaningful farewell for a loved one.

Neil's book is critical to helping Celebrants deliver the best funeral service possible. His knowledge reaches toward the goal of helping every family in need after someone dies.

Neil and I are kin in this incredible work of Celebrancy. While Celebrants shed tears from time-to-time, we try to be strong but connected to sharing the story at hand. This is truly the greatest work we've ever done and we're committed to helping an entirely new generation, as Celebrants are needed in every community, every city, every country, and every continent. Families are grieving and we need more Celebrants. In the States, our numbers are small but the need is great and it is increasing as family members realize the vision of the "perfect funeral" is changing. We cater toward healing whether the service is religious, spiritual or non-religious. We listen and fit the need.

If a family wants to play the decedent's favourite song in a service, the answer is always, "Yes."

If a family wants prayers and scripture, the answer is always, "Yes."

If a family wants to create their own ceremony with a floral tribute, the answer is always, "Yes."

If a family wants to share a story in a service, the answer is always, "Yes."

If the family wants an anecdotal laugh mid-service, the Celebrant had better deliver a heartfelt laugh. How do we learn to do this? Neil's advice will help.

Every funeral service should remind those present that this life mattered. Celebrants intend to leave surviving family members and friends with a legacy that will carry them forward. Doing our homework and fine-tuning our skills will help Celebrants reach this goal.

Funerals are unpredictable as well and you need to be prepared for every scenario. How will we handle the unexpected? Neil offers an honest approach that every Celebrant needs to know before they take the pulpit or stage of their first funeral or their 100th funeral. If you haven't been surprised in a funeral; that day will come.

One of the biggest compliments I receive at the funerals I conduct is from the oldest, most elderly in the crowd: "Honey, thank you so much. That was the best funeral and I could hear every word." We can't mumble if we want to be effective Celebrants. It's not only boring; it's pointless.

Honestly, I am grateful that Neil has taken this incredible approach to help the entire Celebrant community at large in Scotland, the United Kingdom, Australia, and the United States. As we grow in numbers, excellence needs to be the common thread among us. That will set us apart from those who attempt to take on the role as funeral officiant without proper training. Celebrant should not be a title that one can adopt without official training because a family is grieving and they need the best possible person to conduct a funeral that is meaningful.

This book is one that we will keep on our reference shelf, as we'll be re-reading it time and again when approached for a one-of-a-kind funeral that requires personal attention. For a Celebrant to do his or her job effectively, we need to embrace our skills and hone them into fine working tools.

If you are looking for a guide to how to speak at a funeral that is full of passion, you have found the right book.

At the end of the day, if we leave a family smiling at the memories, it is truly a job well done as we proudly wear the title of 'Funeral Celebrant'.

Preface

The purpose of this book is to help Civil Funeral Celebrants improve and become the best possible speakers and Funeral Celebrants. It is written for those already working within the Civil Funeral profession, for those thinking about becoming a Funeral Celebrant and also to help individuals who are suddenly asked by family or friends to deliver a eulogy at a funeral and don't know where to start.

This is the first book of its kind ever to be written in the UK and its author, Neil Dorward, is one of the most experienced Civil Funeral Celebrant in the UK. He is one of only a handful of people in these isles to hold an internationally accredited Diploma in Funeral Celebrancy. He is a trained Professional Speaker and a member of the prestigious Professional Speakers Association.

Neil also trains future Celebrants to embrace the profession with every fibre of their being through the Association of Independent Celebrants (AOIC). The AOIC has recently been awarded the license to deliver the first ever Diploma in Civil Funeral Celebrancy within the UK through the International College of Celebrancy in Australia and is honoured to be facilitating a course devised by the founding father of the Civil Celebrancy movement, Dally Messenger III.

When it comes to speaking at a funeral, the highest standards of excellence should be delivered. Families must be given the best possible funeral service. Neil is passionate about the whole area of speaking well in public and wants to help and support those who speak at funerals to attain these standards. A funeral is arguably the most important day of your life. Families deserve to have someone leading the funeral who is properly qualified, is certified by national standards and is a trained professional speaker. This is a unique form of speaking and even the most seasoned of speakers can find a funeral speech a daunting task.

Perhaps this is why Andy Lopata and Peter Roper entitled their best selling book, 'And Death Came Third'. In 1984 a New York Times survey found there are three things that people fear most in the world. First was walking into a room of strangers, second was speaking in public and death came third.

If these are the three greatest fears in the world, it is fortuitous that this book will help remove the anxiety and fear from doing all three. Civil Funeral Celebrants are, on a daily basis, facing the supposed three greatest fears in the world since they have to walk into a room full of strangers at a crematorium or funeral parlour, and then have to speak to the public about death.

Speaking effectively at a funeral is not as daunting as its sounds. Being a Funeral Celebrant is a wonderfully rewarding job. If you aspire to inspire when someone expires, if you want to become a professional Funeral Celebrant, as well as an effective communicator and a brilliant speaker at end of life ceremonies, then this is the right book for you.

This guide will help you to become an inspiring speaker and will equip you with the right tools to help families at one of the most important occasions in their lives; the funeral.

This book will explain where and why the Civil Celebrancy profession started, and reflects on why young people and the baby boomers are leading the funeral industry towards a new direction of bespoke funeral ceremonies. Increasingly people are demanding that their loved one's funeral (and indeed their own) should be meaningful, celebratory and delivered by powerful and passionate speakers who will ensure that people leave that funeral service thinking, 'that was the best funeral I have ever attended'.

The nature of funeral ceremonies and funerals in general is changing. One of the last taboo subjects is slowly but surely being spoken about. We can see that from recent examples like Patrick Swayze in the USA and the late Jade Goody in the UK, who passed away on Mother's Day, 22nd March 2009. Both of these people spoke openly about their mortality. Death and funerals are becoming a more acceptable topic to discuss. Further chapters within the book make the point that funerals rites and rituals have been around for thousands of years but new trends are emerging, namely the personalised funeral service that celebrates the life of the person who has died rather than just mourning their passing. In Chapters 4, 5, 6 and 7 Neil offers invaluable advice for those who aspire to inspire at a funeral service and ends by inviting people to think about writing their own eulogy in advance as an act of kindness to their family and friends. He also offers two versions of his own eulogy as an example.

What is so unique about Neil is that he was the first full-time Civil Funeral Celebrant in Scotland, has spoken at over 1,500 funerals and has experienced just about every eventuality you will ever find at a funeral. From chief mourners collapsing half way through his eulogy at a crematorium, to people fighting at a graveside, pigeons being released at the end of a service and dropping their 'good luck' charms on the mourners, and Neil still reverentially trying to say the words of final farewell at the moment a coffin gets stuck in a grave and will not go any further. One of his favourite anecdotes concerns a fellow Celebrant who was chatting with a church minister on the telephone arranging a funeral. She happened to mention that she would be more than willing to organise a rush printing job of an Order of Service sheet for a bereaved family. 'No worries', she said to the Minister, 'just deliver them to the nice lady with the ample bosoms'. What she did not know was that her conversation was being broadcasted on the speaker phone to a room full of grieving relatives!

Neil will encourage you in a humorous and thought provoking way to take on board vital speaking tips for a funeral and will inspire you to become the best speaker you can possibly be at a funeral. This is the first book to give you tools, knowledge, insight and guidance into the emerging profession known as Civil Funeral Celebrancy.

Neil receives hundreds of comments, letters and emails from families telling him that what he did for them was deeply moving, exactly how they wanted it to be and is often asked if he will be around to take their funeral. Neil wants to share these insights and tips with you and he will help you speak effectively at a funeral, even the most challenging such as a child's funeral and funerals for families bereaved by suicide and murder.

This book will make a difference to you if you speak at funerals because for the first time ever all the secrets on being a successful speaker at a funeral are shared with you. Neil's reasons for writing this book are to enable the Civil Funeral profession to grow from strength to strength and to give families the funeral they and their loved one deserve. Neil wants to help his colleagues within the profession conform to best practice, and will offer many case examples and stories. It is like no book written and every page contains stories and useful information on how to be a great speaker, aiming to exceed current best practice.

Civil Funerals Celebrants are in a relatively new profession within the UK, arriving about the year 2000. The profession has been flourishing in Australia for over 35 years and the USA for 10 years. Now a guide has been written to help men and women to become the best Funeral Celebrant they can possibly be.

Contents

(Along with some suggested 'Die Tunes' to download for your funeral service)

Chapter 1

Everybody's Talkin' - Harry Neilson

Why is this profession so special?

The nature of funeral ceremonies is changing. I know because I have been hanging around funeral parlours, crematoriums and bereaved families for the last four years of my life and have conducted over 1,500 funerals. I was Scotland's first full time Civil Funeral Celebrant and have officiated at every kind of funeral ceremony imaginable and experienced almost every situation you could find at a funeral.

- Two hearses arriving for two different funerals at the same time

- The wrong songs getting played at the crematorium

- Mourners collapsing in the front row

- A heckler within the congregation who offered a barrage of swear words to me (or possibly the deceased!)

- A punch up as the people left the funeral

- A mobile phone falling out of someone's pocket at the graveside as the coffin was lowered and landing in the grave

- A Church Minister verbally abusing me and telling me what a disgrace I was to the funeral profession. As far as he was concerned, there was not enough religion in the funeral he had just attended (and I had officiated at) despite the fact that the family who put the service together did not want any religion in the ceremony.

Some people say to me, "Isn't it a morbid job, going to funerals every day?" but it is anything but depressing. Conducting funerals is a wonderfully exciting and reflective job. Not many jobs help you to think about the most important things in life. Why are we here on this earth? Why do you do your job? What are you passionate about in life? If you had a near death experience and saw your life whizzing past, would you have any regrets and wish you had done something else with your life? If you won the lottery tomorrow and had no worries at all in life, what would you be doing come Monday morning? Working as a Funeral Celebrant helps me focus on the greatest passions within my life.

This profession is special because we fit the service to people's needs and wishes. It is special because, for most Celebrants, this is our full time job. It is special because many of us are trained professional speakers. Above all, Civil Funerals are special because we craft the right stories and words and create the most meaningful ritual that brings that family to a new place of comfort and healing.

Funerals – A celebration of life

In 99.9% of the funerals I conduct, it is clear that at the end of people's lives, the most important things are not money and material things, but family and friends. When I visit a family to talk about the person who has died and write up their life story, I have never had a request to tell the congregation at the funeral that the deceased wished he or she had more money in their bank account when they died. It is more about the importance of spending real quality time with your children and your parents, eating more ice cream, kicking more leaves in the autumn and making peace with that long lost brother you fell out with 20 years ago. It's funny how, all of a sudden, at the end of our lives and when it comes to what will be said about us when we die we want to remember the good stuff and not dwell on the more awkward stories.

Nowadays people want a funeral service that is memorable and celebratory. To some families a 30-year-old story of a picnic in Burntisland in freezing cold Scotland (that's July by the way) in dad's clapped out old Bedford van, with what felt like half the kids in the street crammed in the back, is a vital memory that must be re-told at the funeral service. It makes perfect sense for the immediate family to want to remember their loved ones in their own way. Why should the family not decide what stories should be recalled on the day of the funeral? If this means that during the same picnic 30 years ago the family remembered the jokes and hilarity in that van and dad drinking a tin of McEwan's Export (thankfully no longer allowed) and that they now understand why two pieces of bread stuck together with jam and consumed at a beach are called a "sandwich", then these stories must be re-told regardless of someone else's opinion of how relevant or interesting that story is. It may be nostalgic and, to the uninitiated, sound sentimental but these are the kinds of things many people want to hear at a funeral nowadays; of some great day 30 years ago with their dad and how they ate candy floss and chips in a poke (bag) on the way home from their day at the beach.

Funerals are a wonderful opportunity for family and friends to remember all the reasons why they loved someone and are going to miss them. For me to be the one who communicates that message at a funeral is a fantastic privilege. The honour of a family inviting you to celebrate the life of someone who had a major (or minor) impact within a family is a great job. Every day I drive to a crematorium or graveside to talk about the dead and my job is to make the dead come to 'life', so to speak. To talk with such authenticity, warmth, compassion and passion that people come to me at the end of the service and say things like; "Are you a friend of the family?", "How long did you know John for?" It is a tremendous honour to speak well of the dead and bring them to life in the hearts, minds and souls of those whose lives were touched by this individual.

I recently conducted a funeral for a man who was a prisoner of war in Germany during World War II. He saw many of his friends die of starvation but amazingly survived the concentration camp. When he returned home to civvy street, he got on with his life. He fell in love, had a family and a successful career and wrote a book about his experiences. He then lost his sight. You might think the war, the Stalag or the inability to see might have put him off life, but not Alan. He was such an inspiring man that it was a privilege to talk about him at his funeral. He oozed positivity throughout life and when I spoke about him at his service in a Dundee hotel and celebrated his life I couldn't help but think, "I should be more like this man. If someone dents my car door in the supermarket car park, is it really worth getting mad about? If children don't eat their brussel sprouts, does that merit me being in a bad mood with them for the rest of the night?" There has been many an occasion when I have conducted a funeral like the one for Alan MacKay, the Daily Record journalist and author of '313 Days Before Christmas' and driven home reflecting on my own life, my wife and children and thought, "I should be more like this…I ought to make more time to do that…why don't I adopt that person's philosophy on life tomorrow." Not many jobs allow you to do that on a daily basis.

Few jobs give this opportunity to reflect on life, why we are here and what is most important. Who else has a vocation and profession where you are given an insight into what makes people tick, into what people want from life, into what drives them on day by day or maybe forces them to give up on life? As a Funeral Celebrant, I am given a wonderful insight into someone's soul and am gifted with someone's life story and treasury. It is noble to speak about the deceased in the best possible way. Not only is a funeral the last ever public act of your life, it is the only time in your life when a disparate group of people come together for an hour, for a unique occasion and then go home their separate ways. When you think about it, how many times will someone stand up in public and speak well of you? Possibly when you retire or at a Silver or Golden Wedding celebration, but there are not many such occasions. All the more reason for a funeral ceremony to be beautifully written and skilfully delivered. It is right and proper to celebrate a life well lived.

Within a typical funeral gathering just think of who is there. Some people will have known John when he played football and scored the winning goal for the school team, others recall the good looking teenager who wooed the girls on his Vespa bought from his first pay packet. Some people only worked with John for a couple of years, saw him at the golf club bar or spoke to him over the back garden wall about the price of fish. All of a sudden, at a funeral, this contrasting group of people come together for a never to be repeated occasion. My attitude therefore is that the deceased and all family and friends deserve the best 'celebration of life' service possible no matter who they were and what they have done or not done in life.

Funerals are wonderful human occasions. They are not always easy; many are tragic and prove the point that life can be unfair. Why should children die? What do you say to a husband whose wife has just died in childbirth? How do you find words to comfort a broken-hearted mother whose son has been murdered in cold blood 10,000 miles away in a foreign country and no one was there to hold his hand? Why should a beautiful 21-year-old girl die of cancer when her whole life was in front of her? What do you say to parents who have to bury their twin babies? What about the family who have had such awful memories of someone who was desperately cruel to them in past years and yet they still have to have a funeral ceremony for that person they may not have liked? How do you find the right words when there are absolutely no positive words or thoughts to share about that person and where some people are delighted the old git is dead? The family will tell you how they want their loved one's life to be celebrated or recalled and what words they need to hear.

Why Civil Funerals?

With statistics telling us that church attendances are declining massively, who will minister to people who may not go to church very often or who have had a negative experience of a funeral and thought "never again"? What if the words and memories you want to talk about are not reflected within the ceremony and you did not get a chance to see a draft copy of the service before it was delivered? That's not right; it's your funeral you should get to see what will be said in advance. What if you are told you are not in control of what will be said on the day of the funeral, the officiant is? Who will give a family the exact service that they want, no questions asked and no judgments made? Civil Funeral Celebrants will.

In February 2008 a leading Church of Scotland Minister, Reverend Johnston McKay, said only regular and faithful church goers should be entitled to have funeral in a church and non attendees should be provided for by other officiants. Until a few years ago the basic choice in the UK was to have a religious funeral in a church or an atheistic (Humanist) service in a crematorium, funeral parlour or at a graveside.

Civil Funerals offer a third option giving families real choice. Properly trained and accredited professional speakers lead these services with less reference to the beliefs of organised religion or the philosophy of the Humanist Society. The beliefs, wishes and values of the deceased and their family are paramount.

Funeral ceremonies in the UK are changing in nature. You should have the right to create the exact service you want when you die, according to your values, wishes and beliefs. Even if your only experience of a funeral is what you have seen on EastEnders, you will know that more and more people are requesting personalised and celebratory funerals. A cursory glance at the newspapers and the internet will reveal that families are making it clear exactly what they want when the time comes for their funeral.

If people wish to find out more about the changing nature of funeral ceremonies I would encourage them to subscribe to a truly magnificent and incredibly comprehensive newsletter from one of America's leading Civil Funeral Celebrants, Pam Vetter, otherwise known as thefunerallady.com. If you dip into her archive of funeral stories you can hear about people's individual needs, wants and wishes and the changing world of funeral ceremonies. The inventor of the Pringle Crisp tube had his ashes placed into a Pringles cylinder. There is the company who can turn your cremated remains into an Hb pencil and the brilliant story of two sons who bought their mum a traffic meter and cemented it next to her graveside stone. Of course the meter said 'just expired'. Pam's newsletter also reports on the incredible story of a man called John Henry Smith who passed away in July 2005. When he died, he was laid out in his local funeral parlour on his favourite recliner chair, wearing his beloved (American) football top - the Pittsburgh Steelers - a can of beer in one hand and a remote control for the television in the other. This rivals the story of the lady in England who wrote in advance how she would like her funeral service. She must have had happy memories of her wedding car with 'Just Married' and the good old tin cans trailing behind it because she let her loved ones know, in advance of her funeral, that the words 'Just Dead' were to be spelt out in flowers in the back of the hearse and her many many shoes were to trail behind the funeral cars.

Increasingly families are advising the funeral industry that they want to be in control of the day when they leave this earth. And why not? Why not, in this day and age, have the funeral ceremony exactly as you would like it? There will always be room for church funerals and Humanist funerals. But what about those who do not go to church and who are not atheists and are somewhere between religion and atheism? Society needs Civil Funerals and professionals who are dedicated to funeral ceremonies.

Google a few sites like mydeathwish.com or mywonderfullife.com and you will see that people are making plans for how they would like to be remembered when they are gone. Perhaps the task of planning a memorable funeral is somewhere in their list of 101 things to do before they die but the fact is, we are in a new age of funeral ceremonies, and Civil Funerals Celebrants are a welcomed profession within the western world because they are leading the way for personalised and bespoke

funeral ceremonies. It seems evident that we need Civil
Funerals because people want them.

The emergence of personalised funerals

Whether we like it or not, we are dealing with a new age
of baby boomers who are not afraid to tell it like it is. They
are requesting tailor-made services. From having Monty
Pythons 'Always Look On The Bright Side Of Life' being
played as people leave their service, to requesting no-
one wearing black at the funeral. Others have even made
arrangements that their loved one will get emails sent to
them from beyond the grave for up to 10 years after they
have passed away. Some people think it is a great idea to
have their ashes collected from the crematorium on the
day of their funeral and sent away to a company who will
turn them into a firework to be set off on Guy Fawkes
Night. They may think it perfectly acceptable to put the
fun into funerals and have a novelty coffin that looks like a
pint of beer or for everyone to come to the funeral dressed
in their favourite football colours. More and more people
are open to funerals being individualised, personalised and
meaningful. I have led hundreds of funeral ceremonies with
live musicians, speeches from people who actually knew
the person, PowerPoint slide shows as well as a prayer, a
hymn and some Frank Sinatra numbers as we entered and
exited the crematorium.

I hear the argument on blogs and web pages that this is
nothing more than egotism gone mad and that over the
top 'celebrations' with football songs and white doves being
released at a funeral is nothing more than the deceased

dictating how they shall be remembered at their memorial service. For some this borders on the side of pomposity, arrogance and the 'me me me' culture.

But consider; some people are not even as fussy as that. It is not always about making the funeral so 'memorable' that people speak about it for days, or for the Celebrant to make sure that the mourners laugh at some past story when John got drunk and made a complete fool of himself at his 21st birthday party and passed out stark naked on a beach near Dundee. (By the way John and Neil are not the same person). At the very basic level, all the family want is for you, the presider of the funeral, to get their name right!

Don't laugh, it still happens. I know of a religious Minister who was asked to conduct a funeral service at Dundee Crematorium and he clearly had not done any homework on the deceased. He turned up with his prayer book and said something along the lines of, "My dear friends, can I please welcome you all here today for the funeral service for Agnes". He spoke for a few minutes saying Agnes this and Agnes that until there was a cough from the front row and a rather gruff voice yelled out, "Excuse me, it's no Agnes, it's Angus". Not only did he get the name wrong, he got the sex wrong. If that had been the funeral of someone in my family, I would have cancelled it there and then, told the people to come back another day or got up and taken the service myself. It is not asking much is it? Even if the person who has died has an almost unpronounceable Polish or Ukrainian name, could the officiant not at least write it phonetically on a piece of paper and say it 20 times before they conduct the service. A funeral should not be a bad experience, at the very least the name should be pronounced correctly and yet such appalling mistakes still happen. Proper 'homework' should be done by the officiant so that all mistakes are minimised. What if someone was referred to during a funeral service as James and yet no-one in the congregation ever knew him as James; he was always Jim or Jimmy? Small mistakes can cause irreparable damage and hurt. Even small changes, small acts of personalisation such as nicknames being used individualise a service and instantly offer a more accurate portrait of the deceased.

Painting a true, authentic and sometimes honest picture of life

Most people want me to speak well of their loved one who has died. Nothing more, nothing less. They want me to tell it as it is, according to the family's wishes and to speak with passion, warmth, authority, compassion, sincerity and artistry. That may at times mean I have to deliver a slightly sanitised version of someone's life story and remove embarrassing tales and it may at times mean a somewhat exaggerated version of what someone is said to have done so that only the good bits are being recalled and celebrated at the service.

There is nothing wrong with highlighting the happy stories of someone's life within a funeral eulogy and down playing the more difficult or challenging times. The family of the deceased do not necessarily want you to tell lies or paint a patently false picture. People are not daft; most people attending a funeral will know a person's good and bad points. The amount of story editing is not the point. The utmost importance is how the deceased's life story is told and the skill of the person speaking during the service.

But at the end of the day it is the family who decide how their loved one will be remembered, they give me the stories and I paint a true and authentic picture of their loved one's life as they see it.

Increasingly families want someone who will turn up at every funeral and give the same quality performance each time; one that touches their heart and soul. The family want to leave the funeral thinking; that was my dad to a tee; you did my son proud; my gran would have loved that or that was the best funeral I have ever attended. People take you into their confidence when you turn up at their family home prior to the funeral to conduct the interview and they want you to move their family and friends on the funeral day, almost make them sit up as they listen to stories about this person they have known and loved. They want to feel inspired on the funeral day.

On many an occasion, when I have conducted an interview, I have witnessed husbands, wives and children open their hearts and reveal intimate secrets for the very first time. Parents may even tell the Celebrant stories they have never told their children before. A life has ended, people have things to say and they want you, the Civil Funeral Celebrant, to re-tell these stories in an engaging and passionate way because that family believes their loved one deserves only the very best. The call for personalised funeral ceremonies is loud and clear.

I remember one lady telling me that she had only just found out that her mother, who was a stunning girl in her early days, had been photographed by the once famous Mayfair magazine. Sons and daughters of another family told me they had only just realised what their mum meant about their dad working in 'Butlins' when they were children. It was actually another type of holiday camp that was run by Her Majesty's Prison Service. Another one of my favourites was the elderly man who went into his garage every day to tinker about. Two years later, when a low level articulated lorry drew up within the Broughty Ferry cul-de-sac, to the disbelief of friends and neighbours, there emerged a magnificent red aeroplane that had been hand built by this incredible octogenarian. His son still flies it to this day at Perth Aerodrome.

Celebrants are gifted someone's life story and are asked to skilfully deliver that story in a way that will make the deceased family and friends feel proud. Is there anything more precious than painting a true and meaningful picture of someone's life?

So what is a Civil Funeral?

Civil Funerals are a relatively new vision of how funeral ceremonies should be conducted. The first was conducted in the UK around about the year 2000. Civil Funerals are not anti religious but they are totally different from atheistic / Humanist ceremonies. Civil Funerals are unique because they can be religious, semi religious or non religious in nature. They do not object to religious content. Their basic premise is that your needs, your beliefs and your values are most important, not ours. They do not preach religion or Humanist philosophy unless of course that is what the family have asked for. It is a job for passionate people, creative writers, eloquent speakers and for people who want to assist families through the bereavement process. It is not uncommon to visit a family and find out that the deceased was an agnostic, his widow a lapsed Roman Catholic and of the three children, one goes to church now and again, one never goes and the third is open to every religion under the sun. It seems to me that only Civil Funerals can serve such families without any risk of compromising anyone's beliefs and values. Everyone's beliefs can be accommodated within a Civil Funeral. This makes Civil Funerals different.

A Civil Funeral is a 'bespoke', 'tailor made' or 'personalised' funeral ceremony and completely different to any other funeral, because every individual is different.

As Dally Messenger III from the International College of Celebrancy in Australia will tell you, when the Civil Celebrancy movement began there in July 1973, the Australian Government had noticed the decline in church attendances and decided the time was right to have ceremonies (initially it was only marriage ceremonies) that reflected people's own choices and preferences.

This was a fundamental cultural change. Prior to 1973 most ceremonies, whether weddings or funerals, were in churches or registry offices. The church or the state was making all 'the rules'. The Australian government was radical. Power was to be taken from the state or church and given to the individual. Ceremonies would no longer be dictated from 'on high' but would be created 'from below', from the people, from the couple to be married, from the bereaved family. It was a realisation that the funeral ceremony is yours; you decide how it will be.

Soon the news of Civil Funerals spread to New Zealand, the USA and the UK and it is predicted to be a service that will grow in popularity as it seems to fit the spiritual, emotional, sociological and psychological needs of many people in the UK today.

Please note, not all Civil Funerals are 'celebrations'. I know the word is commonly bandied about but sometimes that is not the right word. I think, for example, about families and communities in Australia who were devastated by the horrific fires in Victoria in February 2009. Sometimes sadness, mourning, grief and lamentation can be the dominant theme for bereaved families.

What is fundamentally being spoken about here is the right of people to have the exact service they want and for everyone else outside the immediate family to accept these choices without judgement or criticism.

The importance of healing

We all mourn in our own way. Indeed we all heal in our own way and we must not forget the power of funeral ceremonies to heal. If a particular song must be played, play it. If the Celebrant has to tell the story of why Uncle George came to be affectionately known as the 'Grumpy old sod' then that story has to be told. The family knows best. There may be certain 'things' that have to be said and addressed at the funeral because that is what they need to say in order to move on. Maybe the individual died alone suddenly at work and no one was with him. Maybe there are allegations of malpractice in the NHS hospital ward and anger within the family in addition to grief. Maybe there has been terrible abuse in the past or violence or theft of a family's inheritance. There could even be a desire for revenge against the person who took the life of a young man in a car accident. If something needs to be said, let it be said. This is a one-off occasion.

The Celebrant gently and patiently allows the family to talk at the family interview so that the right words are chosen for the service. I also know that when a draft version of the service is sent to a family in advance for them to edit and change, they feel empowered. It is vital, from a holistic bereavement perspective, that the family feel happy with what will be said on the day and are at peace with how their loved one's life will be celebrated before the funeral day arrives.

The words spoken and the way the words are delivered can put people at ease and reduce anxiety. This naturally asks for the appropriate amount of preparatory work, often 8-10 hours. But when the right words are crafted and when the Celebrant delivers the words with expertise and passion you can see and feel the effect it has on the grieving family. They will tell you at the end of the service what you have done for them. You see that in their faces. You feel that in their embraces. You read about it in their thank you letters.

I have spoken at funerals for families bereaved by murder and I know that finding the right words is incredibly important. Do the family want to laugh or cry at the funeral even when their father has been murdered? (See Chapter 6.) It is all to do with relationships of trust and giving people the right service, the right words and the very best delivery of these words. That may mean there is an honest recall of life stories and no hypocrisy or it may mean recalling only happy and special memories and, in the above example, never touching upon the evil that befell that individual.

That is why this profession is so special. The family's needs come first. I am not there to promote myself, to talk about how I feel or to be an entertainer. I am first and foremost a professional speaker and Celebrant helping a family grieve in the right way, in their own way.

Chapter 2

Young At Heart – The Bluebells

From baby boomers to iTunes – How new generations are changing the way we think about funerals.

When I was at school, my friend Gary Gibson (aka Septic Syd) and I relished any opportunity to put on our very cool orange checked lumberjack jackets, splash on some Brut, jump into his lime green coloured Vauxhall Chevette and have an 'eye ball to eye ball' with some lucky girls six miles down the road in the village of Carnoustie in the hope of getting, well…what normally turned out to be a bag of chips and no 'eye ball to eye ball' if you know what I mean. Yeh, I grew up in the age of CBs, Wrangler jeans, Tucker Jenkins on Grange Hill, Quenchie Cups and having a smoochie to Rod Stewart's 'Sailing' at the school disco. While CBs are still being used by forty somethings wearing unfashionable jackets, most young people today communicate on social networks. Often when I have to conduct the funeral of a young person, I am directed to their Bebo or Facebook site. Here friends post messages and talk of their love and their grief.

The IT generation

From a sociological perspective, what we have, in effect, are permanent memory boards and everlasting cyber tomb stones. Tributes, words, pictures, poems and stories that will always be there for the family and friends to view and update. Such spaces are explicit signs to the truth that funerals are changing and that young people are leading the way in which loved ones will be remembered. It won't be through newspaper obituaries but through permanent on line memorial sites.

Social networks are a great way for all people, not just young people, to grieve and remember their friends who have died. Within my work as a Civil Funeral Celebrant I am increasingly dealing with sons, daughters and grand children of the deceased who think differently from their parents and have innovative ideas on how they want to be remembered.

Baby Boomers is a term that is used to refer to a generation of people born between 1946 and 1964 when the troops returned home from World War II. Their thoughts, lifestyle and spending habits have had a major impact on the western economy. Baby boomers and now their children are designing their funerals, telling the funeral profession what they want and some are even locking away their final requests on web sites specifically designed for this need.

The first time I was asked to do a PowerPoint /photo slide show for a young man in a hotel, I was not convinced it would work and the photos would be a distraction from the words that were spoken (or should I say a distraction from me and my words!). How wrong I was. The slide show was a huge hit because the photos themselves spoke and the slide show was right because this is what the family wanted. This was their way of coping and being healed from this terrible tragedy. They knew this person best, they knew many of those who were coming along and how they would appreciate these photos. Who was I to even think that I knew the best way to lead that funeral? Yes, I have tremendous experience in leading funeral services and yes, people do need guidance and direction so that the correct funeral service is crafted but there should always be an element of caution for the Celebrant so that the family's needs not the Celebrant's needs come first. On this particular occasion the family were absolutely right in their decision to have a photographic slide show. The photographs showed this great big smile from a young face that so many people knew and loved and although I had not rehearsed the act of turning round and commenting on the photos, I was able to turn around and look at the photographs whilst talking and referring to his wonderful dress sense, his silly hats and those skinny black jeans he was famous for. On that day, I communicated in a far more effective way than I could ever have imagined because of the photo slide show. On another occasion I was asked to wear a football top instead of a shirt and tie. It may not be to everyone's liking but it worked and as far as the immediate family were concerned it added to the sense of occasion and animated his personality in a way words could not.

Times are changing with funerals. Without making sweeping generalisations, Funeral Celebrants will be arriving at a family home to talk about someone who has died and increasingly the people in that room may be people who care for the environment and what carbon foot print they are leaving behind, who express an interest in what is happening within Dignitas clinics in Switzerland or who have possibly been married for the second or third time, the latter being with personalised wedding vows they wrote themselves.

It is all about choice

Every day I meet bereaved families who want to talk about green burials, wicker basket coffins or make specific requests for everyone to wear something pink at the funeral. In short, this new generation of baby boomers and now their children want to be in control of everything that will happen in their lives from their careers to what will happen to them when they die. As Pam Vetter reports in her newsletter, people are already making plans to be buried at the bottom of the sea in permanent memorial sites or leaving instructions for a sky diver to scatter their ashes to the four corners of the earth, another example you might say of thinking outside the box or blue sky thinking!

I can understand why some people may be slightly uncomfortable with all of these developments. Most of these things were not happening a generation ago. Most funerals followed a fairly typical, predictable and rigid format. But no-one can fail to have noticed society's move away from traditional funeral services to celebration of life services. There has been a shift of focus away from being sad at a funeral to celebrating life. The sadness, the tears and the mourning is not by-passed or ignored, but the over arching theme of the funeral is life rather than death.

Those who work within the world of personal branding remind us that we live in a self obsessed world where everyone is a personal brand. If we take that to its logical conclusion, we can argue that the funeral is the final opportunity to brand and market ourselves. At the funeral of Isabella Blow in May 2007 one of her magnificent hat creations was placed on her coffin because she was the hat diva; that was her brand. Is this just theatre? Are we now reducing the funeral to the level of consumerism and making a personal statement? Some people may think we already have. Maybe we have to ask ourselves why these changes are taking place. I believe it is because we live in a society where people want choice in everything. If you want hats, balloons, bagpipes or a service that has two hymns, two prayers and a benediction you can have it. You can mix and match religion/spirituality and personal tribute in any way you want. It is all about choice.

In my experience of working with bereaved sons, daughters and grand children, although they may not be banging on the church door every Sunday they do have spirituality and they want a ritual that speaks to them. We could argue that the church is at fault here and is even missing out on a great opportunity to evangelise and reach out to those who only occasionally use their services. Why not offer another ritual that nourishes those on the margins, those who are outside the walls of the church? The funeral is one of the most important days in our lives, if not the most important. If churches prepare parents for baptism and tell them what Holy Communion and Confirmation means, why not reach out to the bereaved and comfort those outside the church walls? The beautiful story of Jesus dialoguing with the woman at the well (Gospel of John Chapter 4) makes the point that sometimes you have to meet people where they are in life.

Today there are many articles in newspapers and on the internet about the death of the traditional funeral and the emergence of this next generation of personalised ceremonies. The terminal illness and subsequent death of the Big Brother celebrity Jade Goody was headlines news through the first few months of 2009 and she let it be known that she wished her funeral to be conducted exactly as she wanted it. Sure there was a high celebrity factor here but she still planned her funeral service and told her family and the funeral industry what she wanted. It is all about choice.

I know from my many years within this profession that part of the reason why some individuals are requesting pop songs, poems and personalised services is that they feel traditional rituals have failed to comfort them. Previous experiences of funerals have on other occasions led people to believe they will never be healed by the conventional funeral words and rituals. Some Ministers and Priests are very accommodating to such requests (for pop songs, poems etc.) but not all. There are many excellent church Ministers and Priests and they touch peoples hearts and souls not only with the ritualistic words but how the words are delivered. However first hand accounts from bereaved families tell me this can be hit or miss and that people are making choices to go elsewhere for the funeral. If someone has not been to church in many years or the Vicar in the local parish has changed several times how will the bereaved family know their funeral service will be conducted as they want it? This is what people increasingly want; a funeral service conducted according to their needs and beliefs. I see both sides to the debate here. People want change and a personalised funeral and sometimes the church say, 'but listen there is only so much we can change'. There was a recent story about a Priest who lamented the day a family wrote to his Bishop and complained because the grand daughter could not dance at the funeral. Quite right, church services should be religious and often the liturgy cannot be changed but that doesn't mean that an alternative kind of service cannot be offered, and people's funeral wants are listened to.

I know from ten years of experience working with young adults that people between the ages of 20 – 40 who are bereaved say by the death of a parent, are increasingly telling the Minister or Priest; "this is what I want" and I do not see this trend changing at all. Some Ministers and Priests will listen to these requests, others will not. Those who feel they are not being listened to are increasingly going elsewhere for the funeral ceremony or, on the flip side, are choosing church services for reasons other than religion.

I conducted a funeral of a young man and there was a debate within the family about whether the funeral should be in the church or the Funeral Directors parlour. The centre of the debate was not whether the gentleman was a church goer or was baptised (which he was), the central question for the family was: Will the funeral parlour be big enough? It wasn't, so they had the service at the church, against the wishes of the gentleman, who made it clear to his brother he did not want a church service but this was over-ruled because the local church was the only space big enough to accommodate the large crowd. The funeral took place in the church not for religious reasons but due to the size of the building. It again makes the point that families increasingly want to be in charge of the funeral service.

People are willing to state what they want and do not want and I believe Civil Funerals will increasingly take centre stage within the UK and within the next generation. I predict that Civil Funerals will be the dominant funeral service that families will request within the next generation. Civil Funerals have been in existence in Australia for some 36 years and Civil Celebrants conduct 60% of all funerals in Australia. There are approximately 8000 Civil Celebrants working in the profession in Australia conducting funerals, marriages, baby namings and other civil ceremonies.

The use of humour

In addition to making funerals meaningful and memorable some people want to put the fun into funeral. That is ok if that is what the family is looking for however I still believe a respectful line will always be drawn. Civil Funerals are not an 'anything goes' ceremony. They are not a dumbing down of bereavement or frivolous ceremonies. They are authentic, sincere, meaningful and moving ceremonies that match people's spiritual and emotional needs. A

Funeral Director I work with jokingly suggested to me that he could see the day when a cowboy loving Scotsman, who occasionally frequented the bucking bronco bars in the USA would ask for the Civil Celebrant to ride on top of a coffin that has been placed on to the mechanism of a bucking bronco whilst shouting 'yee ha'. This isn't going to happen. A funeral is not a fairground, there is true mourning, sadness and grief and this is always respected, but times are changing and we need to talk about the funeral.

Trends within the industry are undoubtedly shifting. Some Funeral Directors offer hearses and funeral cars that are gold in colour while one English company even has a fleet of converted VW Beetles. Some people are paying thousands of pounds to have their loved one's ashes turned into a real diamond and others will say it is ok to release balloons at the funeral of a baby. Civil Celebrants fit the service to the family.

This doesn't mean there must be fireworks and balloons and the release of white doves if that is not how you would like your mum to be remembered. Nor is humour and laughter a must. There are many guides on the internet on how to write a eulogy (see Chapter 7) and some will say that humour must be injected, but I profoundly disagree with that thought. Sometimes humour is not relevant, for example, at a baby's funeral or for someone who frankly just wasn't funny. Never throw in humour during a funeral service just for the sake of it. Everyone has a different interpretation of what makes a meaningful funeral. It is a combination of honour, grief, respect, celebration, reverence, mourning and saying farewell. What is true is that families are deciding what is appropriate for them and what kind of service will truly aid their mourning and grieving.

Writing your own eulogy

If we were to be honest, we would accept the truth that most of us do not think about our funeral ceremony on a daily, weekly or even monthly basis. How we would like to be remembered when we no longer exist is not what motivates most people. Although many successful business people like Steve Jobs at Apple Mac argue that awareness of our mortality is the greatest motivational tool ever and although we know in our heads that death will come to us all one day, most people don't think about their funeral and just go about their daily lives.

In December 2007 a 35-year-old-man went to his work in Motherwell. I am not sure what he did that Saturday morning he woke up. Maybe he had egg on toast, kissed his wife and kids, jumped in his car and went off to earn a living. I bet you he didn't wake up that morning of 29th December thinking about his funeral and what would be said about him at his funeral by the newspapers and former work colleagues. But after 72 minutes on the playing field at Fir Park, Phil O'Donnell the captain of Motherwell Football Club dropped dead whilst doing his job as a footballer. Tomorrow is promised to no-one.

What if you knew you were going to die today? Would that change your life? Would it make you think not only about what would be said on the day of your funeral but who would do the talking? Then imagine you could hear what was being said at your funeral. Imagine you could read your own obituary. Worse still imagine you didn't like what was being said. The legendary singer Tom Jones read his obituary some time in November 2008 after false rumours about his death, as have Tom Cruise, Mark Twain and many others. In September 2008 John Delaney, who was reported dead in 2003, 'reappeared' five years after his son said goodbye to him, or somebody, at his funeral. A case of mistaken identity still resulted in his son John mourning his father or mourning someone who was cremated that day in 2003 when that funeral took place.

If we took time to answer some of the questions about how we would like to be remembered at the end of our lives then we will have a better idea of the kind of ceremony we would like. The man who was reported dead but was not can look at his life differently and may already be making plans for what will be said about him at his real funeral. This man is one of the few people in the world who can re-write his funeral eulogy. What would you do if you were given another chance to re-write history? Seriously, when it comes to your funeral, how would you like to be remembered? What if you could have a say on the matter?

It is a sombre point and young people are leading the way. There are web sites encouraging people to write their own eulogy and have it safely locked away until it is needed. These sites even allow you to update it and re-write it as often as you wish.

In addition to writing my own Will and deciding who's getting my original yellow label Beatles albums to sell on eBay, I have written a couple of pages on how I would like to be remembered at the end of my life and I have stapled these pages on to my Will just in case I die tomorrow and they are also available in Chapter 10 of this book. If there is one thing I would encourage all people to do, it would be to take some time to write a couple of pages of A4 on how they would like to be remembered at the end of their life and safely file it away.

As a Funeral Celebrant I am, in effect, telling your life story from the perspective of your family and on most occasions the deceased has no input since most people do not write their life story down in advance or even scribble on a beer mat the basic points of how they want to be remembered. It is presumed by most of us that on the day of our funeral we will like what is going to be said about us.

I remember growing up in the small village of Monifieth near Dundee and my father sat me down in the living room one day next to the paraffin heater. He coughed and shuffled a bit and then started talking about his early days growing up as a boy in our village and how it was his job to bring the coal into the house to earn his pocket money. I must admit I wasn't paying attention too much at this point, I was trying to solve a Scobby Doo mystery but he blurted out the following words: 'Son, do you know what sex is?' My face went as red as the fire we were sitting next to. 'Son,' he said, 'sex is what posh people from Broughty Ferry get their coal delivered in.' I never understood the sacks of coal joke till many years later but it makes the point that just as parents used to feel awkward about talking to their children about sex, so children can feel awkward about talking to their parents about death. Your mum might not jump up and down with joy if you buy her a plot at the local cemetery for her next birthday but it is an act of love to sit down with her one day and help her write her life story and articulate how she would like to be remembered.

We need to talk about the funeral

The funeral is possibly one of the last taboo subjects and if any group of people are willing to talk about funerals and death it will be the families of the baby boomers. Signs of this discussion are around. In the British soap opera Coronation Street, a story line that ran in the latter part of 2008 concerned a widow called Emily Bishop. She began to make her funeral wishes known to her friends in 'the street' but one of them, the hilarious sweetie wifie Norris, found the subject of Emily's funeral rather uncomfortable. One episode sees Emily singing the hymn, 'The King Of Love My Shepherd Is' whilst she was in her back garden trimming her lavender bush. Norris asked why she was singing that song and was told by Emily this was the song she wanted to be sung at her funeral. He was uncharacteristically tongue tied and immediately changed the subject from funerals to lavender bushes. It neatly showed that some people are willing to talk about funerals while for other it is an area that should be left alone.

But if you take time to write out some kind of legacy statement at least when the day comes your immediate family will know your wishes because you have articulated them. Angel Pantoja Medina of Puerto Rico apparently told his mum that when his funeral day came he was not to be put into a coffin but propped up in the corner of the living room with his sunglasses on and his baseball cap. He sadly died and his request was granted because he had informed people this is what he wanted.

There are lots of choices these days as to what type of funeral service you have and who leads the service. There are even a small number of people who do not want funerals at all, who do not want any words spoken and where they will be the only person present. It is all about choices and preferences.

I can understand why some people are uncomfortable with the whole nature of funerals becoming more personalised. To some people this is sacrilegious, to others just wishy-washy drivel. But like it or not personalised funerals are on the increase, this is what many people want and if those who lead funeral ceremonies refuse to listen or try to impose their will, people will go elsewhere, particularly if their wishes were made explicitly clear.

What is uplifting and meaningful for one family may seem like the worst funeral ever to another. I was once asked to conduct a two minute funeral. That's what the family told me they wanted and needed. They were very specific about what should be said and what should not be said. When I met the family in their home my immediate thought was 'no you can't have this', then I remembered, it's not about me, it's about them, so the family got a two minute funeral. A couple of weeks later I received a lovely hand written note from one of the children in the family thanking me for the wonderful service and in addition to my fee there was £25 worth of gift vouchers enclosed within the card.

There will be resistance to this call to change the way we think about funerals. Three times in my professional career I have been verbally attacked by clergy. On all three occasions the clergymen were mourners in the congregation and I was verbally abused because, in those particular funerals, there was little use of Sacred Scripture (remember this decision to omit Scripture was the family's choice). I was told at the end of the service, by the clergymen, that what I was doing was despicable. One told me I should be ashamed of myself for having such a job and on one occasion I was told this was the worst funeral he had ever been to. The attack itself was a dent to the old ego and did knock me, especially when they refused to shake hands with me. But the last time I was chastised in public by a man wearing a dog collar, I was a bit more prepared. On this occasion I directed the church Minister to the widower and asked him to repeat his comments to the grieving family about what a terrible funeral it was, needless to say he did not say anything.

What a cheek, attending a funeral and criticising the family who approved a service that they decided was the most meaningful to them. You can make it as religious, semi religious or non religious as you want, don't let anyone tell you otherwise. I was once asked to help hand out tea bags at the end of a funeral because the man who died thought it was funny and wanted everyone to 'have a drink on him'. That old joke may not have been to my own personal taste, but who am I to comment and condemn? I actually preferred the service of a man who predicted that very few people would come to his funeral. He was right, there were maybe 25 people there but what these friends did not know is that at the end of the service every woman would receive a beautiful bunch of flowers and every man a nice bottle of whisky. Your funeral, your choice.

When I think about those who condemn personalised funerals or services they do not approve of, I could never envisage anyone from the baby boomer generation or their children directly or indirectly telling a family they are mourning in the wrong way or in a way they disapprove of. Young people are much more open-minded and tolerant of all beliefs and faiths. Of course there will be occasions when the Civil Funeral Celebrant will encounter complex family dynamics; family members not speaking to each other or people being banned from funerals. I have even had three wives in the front row and have been asked to deliver very honest and almost disturbing words about ruined lives, broken childhoods and seemingly bad people. If that is what the family wants, let them have it. I have been told to brush aside any references to things like time spent in jail, affairs and violence within the home. I will do all of this and more because the family's needs come first.

The latest evidence from Australia (survey by the National Funeral Directors Association in 2009), the birth place of the Civil Celebrancy movement states that:

- 13% of adults want a traditional funeral ceremony

- 68% would like to customise their funeral

- 75% want to arrange their own service in advance

The baby boomers ░░░░ ays wanted to be slightly different from their ░ ░░ nd have things their own way. They do not feel tied or constrained by tradition and the above evidence seems to suggest they will increasingly request personalised funeral ceremonies.

Individualised funeral services will be asked for because we are living in a culture of choice. I know from my experience in the profession that families are not afraid to tell you what they want and be different. Increasingly the focus is less on memorialising death and more on celebrating life. These people are not irreligious nor do they lack spirituality, all they want is some personal touches that speak to them and heal them on the funeral day. We all have choices in life and lots of people are choosing to have a funeral that reflects the way they lived life. This movement towards bespoke funerals may even be a new stage of the bereavement process, who knows? But what is sure is that Civil Funerals are a response to people's expectations, needs and wants. That is why they are a welcomed addition to UK society.

Chapter 3

Spirit In The Sky – Dr and the Medics

Why have rites and funerals anyway?

We need funeral rites and rituals because we are people who think in stories and because we need healing during times of change.

Story

Human beings have been storytellers since the dawn of creation. Oral traditions, such as the story of William Wallace here in Scotland, still survive to this day. Although this particular story has been blurred by legend and myth, we all love stories. That's why soap operas, Bebo and Facebook are so popular, they all communicate real life human stories. What people love about stories is the fact that they unite us and offer a common focal point. They can also be a powerful tool for healing; Alcoholic Anonymous use stories as a way to unite people and heal.

People love to hear stories of the deceased at a funeral as it creates connections, familiarity and commonality. I see people on a daily basis smile, laugh and nod at funerals as I recall what an individual did as a child, how he met his wife, how he felt when he got a hole in one on the golf course and so forth. On a deeper level, stories invite you, the listener, to engage your imagination and faith.

You just need to mention the phrase 'Once upon a time' and instantly your world is connected to the storyteller's world. This is no different to going into work the next day or texting someone and saying; 'did you hear about so and so last night and what they got up to'. We naturally think in stories and from a ceremonial point of view stories must be used within a funeral, provided the stories have relevance and meaning.

A friend of mine went to a Civil Funeral for the first time last year and thought it was awful because the Celebrant referred to the lady's great baking skills and her delicious apple pie. He couldn't understand why anyone would talk about such things at a funeral. The answer is obvious. He didn't know the lady well enough to understand the context and relevance of that story within the family. I fully comprehend why some people would never entertain such memories being spoken about during a church service because the leaders of religious services are first and foremost there to tell biblical stories of faith and hope. There is even a specific ruling within the Catholic Church that there should be no eulogy and sharing of personal memories of the deceased during the Mass and that such reflections should only take place the night before at what is called 'The Reception of Remains'.

It is a different form of storytelling that takes place within a Civil Funeral but it is still storytelling. It is just that we have two different audiences with different needs, wants and personal preferences. The issue for both the clergy and Celebrants is how to mix the two aspects of religions and personalisation. The Humanists are fine, religion is never mentioned but there are many who have faith who still want some personalisation within their church service and there are many people who choose a Civil Funeral and still want to talk about heaven, life after death, want to sing the 23rd Psalm or have a prayer said. Sometimes religious components are needed within the Civil Funeral ritual to authentically re-tell the individual's life story.

We all love stories. Adam and Eve, David and Goliath, Lazarus in the tomb, The Princess and the Pea, Shrek, granny's amazing apple pie. That's what funerals do; they make connections to stories and people in our past. Stories still feed and nourish us.

During 2008, I completed the Diploma in Civil Funeral Celebrancy from the International College of Celebrancy in Australia. If you ever get a chance to study the Australian course designed by the 'father' of the Civil Celebrant movement, Dally Messenger III, you will hear Dally wax lyrical about one of his favourite anthropologists, Arnold Van Gennep and his seminal work 'Les Rites De Passage'. He is the one accredited with coining the term 'Rites of Passage' and to this day it is still an important text for all students of Social Anthropology. Van Gennep observed that most cultures have rites of passage processes that are tripartite in nature. Van Gennep explains this, as separation-transition-incorporation. The basic point being made here is that rites of passage, like funerals, shape our sense of belonging and identity. That is why we love to hear stories at funerals; they provide a sense of identity and cohesion. A funeral is a unique sociological phenomenon and a well prepared and skilfully delivered funeral rite is good for the family and society in general. Please do not think that a 100-year old seminal work in anthropology has little or no relation to our age because it does. The day after the inaugural speech by President Barack Obama on 20th January 2009 it was noted in the chat rooms of the International College of Celebrancy that Barack Obama's speech was pure Van Gennep; it was all about separation, transition and incorporation.

As Dally Messenger will confirm, the psychological function of a passage rite and storytelling is to reduce the stress of change. All change induces fears and anxiety but when there is an appropriate ritual and support structure for the individual to move from one realm to another then the ritual itself can have enormous psychological benefits and, in the case of a funeral, be incredibly nourishing and healing. If that means hearing the story of granny's apple pie or re-telling the story of the mum who went to a fancy dress party in a white sheet with a piece of cardboard sellotaped to her feet (the cardboard had orange flames painted on it) and she called herself 'Death warmed up', then tell that story if it offers healing and comfort to the family.

Funeral Celebrants are not grief counsellors but they see the power of story to help grieving people heal and move on. They see the power within the family's eyes on the funeral day. They see the power of words and their delivery touching people's souls. That is why Chapters 4, 5, 6 and 7 are dedicated to the art of public speaking. No-one has a right to say that a story of grandma's apple pie cannot be recalled at a funeral service.

Healing and pastoral care

Those who lead funeral services are in a special place because they can aid the grieving and healing process through story telling and using the right words. I have read poems for people who have been abused during their childhood and read hand written letters from mothers as they wept bitterly over the coffin of their new born child.

This is a wonderful job. I am offering comfort, closure, healing, dignity, and meaningful words. I am invited to be part of their precious lives for a few days and I know, I truly know, that what I say and how I say it, makes a real difference to people's lives.

At times I am invited in to people's hearts as well as their home and the pastoral care that I extend is therapeutic and spiritually nourishing. It is more however than the words spoken on the day. The power to deliver the words that touch people's hearts is immense, it is real. Pastoral care is more than nice words being said at the funeral and is something that can only be felt, it is about relationships of trust with the family. It comes from a genuine sense of care and wanting to sincerely help families through bereavement. It starts at the first telephone call, the first handshake, the first smile and eye contact and continues with the family interview and the emails and further phone calls. The pastoral care is felt through empathetic words, a compassionate heart and eyes that can speak to another person's soul. It is a privilege to be part of someone's healing process.

Of particular importance within the healing process is allowing the families to know that they are in overall charge of everything. I have found that allowing the family to see a full draft version of the service in advance of the funeral empowers them. Some officiants do not show the family the full draft in advance and only email the main eulogy in the belief that they want to family to have an element of surprise on the funeral day with the specially crafted words they have created for the day. That is ok as long as you have told the family there will be an element of surprise and they have agreed with this. If you do not ask them, you do not know and even though it is small, it is still you controlling part of the ceremony and you deciding the family will like a surprise. They might not. To avoid that scenario I email the entire service to the family. Now they are in control of what will be said on the day. It's really simple, just email the family a copy of the service as soon as you have created it and give them a few days to add, delete or change anything in it. Once the script is right and approved by the family, what I guarantee as a speaker is that I will speak well, and I will bring their loved one to 'life' in a manner of speaking. It is so important that the family are the final editors of the script. I want them to know they can trust me to do my very best for them and I will skilfully deliver their words. I cannot take away their tears, indeed I would not want to, but I can make a massive positive impact on their grief and bring peace to their lives. A well prepared and eloquently delivered funeral can do marvels for grieving families; so much so, I sometimes feel I am like the family Celebrant.

The family Celebrant

In days gone by families were visited by the Parish Priest and the local Minister for births, marriages and deaths. This is changing, not just parish visitation but families choosing who they want to lead their ceremonies. I can see the emergence of what, in essence, will be Parish Celebrants. Already in Australia families turn to the same Celebrant for birth, marriage and death rituals. There are other Civil Celebrants offering adolescent rites of passage ceremonies and pet funerals. Families come back to the same Celebrant time and time again because they know they will get the same quality of service that they want and deserve. I can think of one family for whom I have conducted over 12 funerals in four years. It has now reached the point where they inform me of a death in their family before they phone the Funeral Director. I have several families who now only want to use me for all the significant moments in their family's lives; the hatches, the matches and the dispatches. These are significant changes within society. Families are choosing their own 'minister', in the general sense of that word, to care for them when they need it.

A similar trend has been seen in those who are diagnosed with terminal illness. On many occasions I have been contacted by people who, having been told they have a shortened life expectancy want me to write their eulogy in advance. I have conducted interviews in hospices with very alert people who are terminally ill. It is often a moving and humbling experience, listening to people's last thoughts and words. When these words are delivered at a funeral a few weeks later, the impact is even more powerful because you have the genuine words of farewell which came from that person's heart.

It is not just the terminally ill. Others decide to write their funeral in advance for family reasons. I know of one lady in her late 70s who is as sharp as a tack and has one son in Australia, one daughter in South Africa and no other family here in the UK. The funeral service has been typed up in advance by myself, shown to her several times for her approval and is now safely stored away for her funeral day. It is one of the final acts of love she can offer to her family. Her reasons for doing this were simple. She wanted to spare her son and daughter, who lived far away, any undue worry and anxiety when she passes away.

Human beings need rituals, we need story, and the greeting card industry has shown that we need the right words for the right circumstances. People who are writing their services in advance are saying, "I want to be in charge of my death, I want to be in control of my own destiny, I want my ritual to be as I want it, I want to know what will be said about me when I am gone." I once lead a funeral service that lasted one hour and five minutes, it was full of music and poems and personal reflections. The lady created her own ritual; one she thought would speak to her family. Every word was written out by her and I simply had to express her inner thoughts when it was delivered at her funeral. Not everyone would want their funeral service to go on for over an hour but at least she took control of her own ritual. The young woman spent weeks writing her own tribute and choosing her favourite songs and poems.

Although a long service, it was a poignant and memorable service. The order of service brochures that she designed were magnificent and contained 12 pages of photographs.

What that example shows is that the funeral ritual has to fit the personality of the individual and speak of them. Some families are taking this further and are finding their own family spokespersons or family celebrants. During times of change people seek certainty and reassurance. They want consistency and someone they can rely on. I am convinced this is one of the reasons why Civil Funerals Celebrants are increasing in popularity because they consistently offer the correct rituals and words that families need at major times of change like death.

For most people death is emotionally devastating. In 99% of the funerals I conduct there are genuine tears, grief, sadness and loss. This is always acknowledged with the services I conduct even though the overall tone is one of highlighting the good and happy memories, sometimes these special memories are peppered with honesty and humour. I have conducted several ceremonies for people who have done some pretty bad things in their life and for people who might not be missed that much after death, but there is always an element of change and letting go. Death is all about accepting a new reality, letting go and never seeing that person again, despite feelings and emotions and it is my job to create the ritual that matches all these needs.

That is why the Civil Funeral ritual, the creative way the words are put together and how the words are delivered by the Celebrant is vital in helping people to cope with death. I believe that the most valuable part of the funeral ceremony is how the carefully crafted words are delivered and how they speak to the heart and souls of the listeners and move them on the day.

I got a round of applause at a funeral after telling the following story about a young man's fishing trip with his friends.

As is the tradition for some casual fishermen in Scotland, the men arrived at the quayside with a few tins of beer and went on their merry way to fish. After a few large waves some of them felt a bit worse for wear and leaned over board to feed the seagulls with a recently consumed curry. Only someone who shall remain nameless, while he was chucking up, lost his false teeth in the sea. While most people were panicking about what do next, one quick thinking lad (his name was inserted here), who was ever ready for a laugh no matter the situation, convinced another one of the men to get his false teeth out so they could be tied to his fishing rod and cast over board. During all the commotion the fishing line and false teeth were directed into the sea without any of the other fisherman realising what was going on. Then came the cry and please excuse the vernacular here as this is an exact quote of what was said: "For F***'s sake! Look what I've caught?" Now, the man who lost his teeth is delighted to be reunited with his gnashers and gleefully sticks them in his mouth until he suddenly realises that they don't fit as they aren't his. So he took them out his mouth and threw them back in the sea. Now two men on the ship have no teeth for the next 48 hours. Priceless.

You could genuinely see the people in the congregation belly laugh when that story was re-told in full Technicolor. I can honestly say that the impact was due to:

- Giving the family the correct ritual

- How the story was recounted that day (through good voice tones)

- How it connected to people's memories

- How the words were animated (in the above example I mimicked the fishing rod action as the false teeth we brought on board)

- How I used my body language

This is why I got a round of applause. I was not looking for it, nor was I out to entertain but the story demanded that it was re-told in its full glory, with body language to show I was living the words, otherwise it would have been just words.

"Every time we say goodbye we die a little", so says the Ella Fitzgerald song, we cry a little because something which was precious and valuable to us is no longer here in a physical sense, but that doesn't mean we can't laugh and share some favourite stories and create a ritual that is tailor made to that person. Some people will want three poems in their service, others none. Some will want a 20 minute tribute and a prayer while others will want two hymns and for their best friend to read the eulogy. The ritual has to be created for every individual service since we are all unique.

It is true, that funerals can be immensely sad, that tears can be therapeutic and that a husband can die a few days later of a broken heart after burying his wife. Psychologists will even tell you that grief can induce depression, end marriages and relationships, cause psychosomatic illness and inhibit sleeping patterns but grief is normal, just like laughing and story telling. Most of the Civil Funeral rituals I create have a personalised eulogy that lasts anywhere between 2 and 22 minutes. Sometimes I can have tears rolling down my cheeks as people tell me stories from their loved one's life to be included within the main eulogy. It is an amazing privilege to offer the right words within the right ritual. I once began a eulogy with these words.

"As many people will know Alice was born on the glorious 12th, twelfth of August 1934, which of course meant that Eric was able to legally shoot Alice."

In Scotland the glorious 12th refers to the beginning of the grouse shooting season. The tribute then went on to say these words and, as you read them, ask yourself about how you might have delivered them to gain maximum impact on your audience.

"Seriously, Eric could have shot Alice should she do something like; melt her new boots next to an open fire and used Eric's pint of beer to put out the molten plastic; come flying down the ski slope, land on Eric's head and force his ear into the snow causing him great pain; pour him a cup of coffee from her flask, miss, and scald his hand, hit a pylon at the ski lift whilst trying to read a notice that ironically said: 'Stay clear of the pylons' and have all three emergency services

arrive at the family house because she answered the phone whilst trying to light the coal fire with a sheet of newspaper and subsequently set the chimney on fire. I mean under any one of these circumstances you might say that anyone was entitled to invoke the rights of the glorious 12th."

And there's more,

" She was the kind of girl who could force a local tribal chief in Nigeria to hand over the food she had collected (and he had pinched) and give it back to the people who needed it in the first place; she could charm a senior officer in the Royal Navy to break all the rules and flash Eric's ship, HMS Whitby, as it sailed up the River Forth with a lighted Morse code message that had to be given to Eric in person from his Commanding Officer on the bridge.

We also know about her accident prone ways and how Alice innocently asked an Iranian pharmacist for some glycerine to soften the icing on Alan's pool table cake for his 21st birthday but he gave her nitro glycerine. Now that would have been a party that went off with a bang."

It is perfectly natural for families to want to share great stories. There is nothing wrong with both laughing and crying at a funeral. Although much of the laughter and the tears ride on how the Celebrant constructs the ritual and delivers the words.

As human beings, we need rituals to bring perspective to our lives, especially at some of the greatest transitional periods of our lives. Death brings massive emotional, physical, social and psychological change. A well prepared service can be cathartic, it can help remove guilt and anger and help people move on with their lives.

Chapter 4

Say Hello, Wave Goodbye – David Gray

The basics of being a great Civil Funeral Celebrant.

If there is such a thing as five golden rules for a Civil Funeral Celebrant, they would be as follows:

1. The family's values, needs and wishes come first. We do as they ask. We are at their service, full stop; providing what they ask of us is not illegal or immoral. For example, I usually refuse to say the full blown version of offensive swear words. If a family asks me to swear, I will do so provided there is context and relevance to its use.

2. A Celebrant should never fail to turn up for a funeral or it may well be their last one. If a Funeral Celebrant were in some serious situation (an accident, a snow storm, or sudden illness two minutes before the service begins) they should still pull out all the stops to get another Celebrant and contact the Funeral Directors on their mobile phone to let them know what is happening. In the summer of 2008 I almost lost my voice. I let the family and the Funeral Director know in advance, asked the crematorium to turn up the

volume on the microphone, made a personal choice not to sing the hymn that day and made arrangements that if I could not get through the service a Funeral Director would take over.

3. A Civil Funeral Celebrant is a professional speaker and has the same kudos as any artist, poet or musician. The basic mind set is to never give a lazy or sloppy service. Every 'show' must be the best and to consistently be the best.

4. At the same time, all speakers and Celebrants must be humble enough to realise that they can become better and improve in some way. There is no short cut to a best practice funeral ceremony.

5. A Celebrant must be authentic. When they hear people say at the end of the ceremony 'Thank you, that was the best funeral I have ever attended. Tell me - how long have you known Bob for?' and they admit, 'Well actually I didn't know him', then they will know they are doing something good and worthwhile with their lives. While it is true that some mourners will always say 'lovely service' no matter how average your performance was, be grateful for the compliments.

Skills of a Civil Funeral Celebrant

1. Diplomacy

Imagine the family you meet for the first time within the family home have not come together as a complete family in 20 years. It could be the case that some people may not have spoken to each other for a long time; some may even dislike each other intensely. You could even find there is one individual in the room who hogs the conversation for the entire hour and a half and no-one else gets a word in edge ways.

Funeral Celebrants are called on to be sensitive and diplomatic in the presence of complex family dynamics. I once visited a family where the deceased was bad mouthed by one person in the room and called every 'F', 'C' and 'B' swear word you could imagine. On the interview day, no one in the room objected to the person saying these things, in fact they all laughed (nervously I now see) and went along with what was being said. For the first time ever, and thankfully the only time in 1500 family interviews, I felt very uncomfortable in this house because the young man who had died was having his character and personality run down and torn to shreds and no one in that room defended him or said anything pleasant about him. It was quite horrific. On top of that, this denigration of character took place in front of his young daughter who sat mute on the sofa, just listening.

I went home that night unsure how to start writing the service and while I was writing, the girlfriend of the young man who had died phoned me to apologise for the person who had been downright vicious and thoughtless. She asked me to disregard everything he had said and to write a more positive tribute to the father of her daughter. Thankfully, this was how I was writing it anyway.

Although it is the Celebrant's job to translate the family's stories and memories and never ever judge or criticise what is being said by the family during the interview, it was clear on this occasion that what was being said was venomous, highly inappropriate and more than likely an untrue picture of the person who had died. On such very rare occasions we can question the family on the appropriateness of stories and it would, in my opinion, be prudent to ask the family discreetly if this is really what they want to be recalled on the day of the funeral. In that particular scenario, I came to realise that this one individual was clearly making other people fearful to speak up and was a bully.

It is very rare for families to wash their dirty linen in public and want to bad mouth the dead person in the course of a funeral service, no matter how 'bad' they were. We are not there to judge, we are there to be polite, sensitive and diplomatic and yet no one deserves to be castigated in public, regardless of what they have done.

2. Creativity

A Civil Funeral Celebrant is asked to talk about a person in a creative and entertaining way. The whole service, particularly the eulogy should read and feel like a story, one written in a non chronological way. A story that people want to listen to because it is written well and delivered well, a story that comes from the heart and a story that brings that person alive in a very real sense.

I would argue that it is very important to write and speak in what you might call the family's local language. A tribute is not normally read in the Queen's English nor should it read like a Times Obituary. A Celebrant has to be very skilled in engaging the family at the right level. That does not necessarily mean writing the whole service in broad colloquial language but it should make use of the family's localised accents and words that are particular to their family.

I often use down to earth words, broad Scots, very localised sayings and Scottish sayings like 'eh' and 'ken'. Recently at a funeral I said, "Not that we are saying Wull was thrifty or techt or onything (not that we are saying Will was thrifty or tight or anything) but, as Ella said the other day; 'he wouldna spend a penny if a haw-penny will dae." (He would not spend a penny when half a penny would do) and later on I said, "Och day bother yirself aboot me", which means 'oh don't bother yourself about me." It was a phrase this particular man often said to his family and it meant a lot. That is the basic point. Write about the important stuff and when appropriate, deliver sentences and phrases in that dialect. The Celebrant should speak in a language that speaks to the family and engages them at their level.

For some Celebrants this may cause a sense of unease and appear false but it all depends on how you deliver the words. For example, a family may tell you they are "very prood o' thir di". This is a typical phrase that may be used in a part of Scotland known as Fife and it means the family was "very proud of their granddad". It is simply a case of tapping in to your audience's background and writing in an engaging almost entertaining style. Not necessarily 'entertaining' as in 'ha ha ha' but entertaining as in, 'for the next 20 minutes folks you really will want to listen to me telling you the fascinating life story of this person you knew and loved'.

3. Reliable

A good Funeral Celebrant should be consistent in his or her standards of excellence and should be a highly competent speaker every time. They should not bring unnecessary attention to themselves and they should certainly not give the impression that the funeral service they have just delivered that day is the same one they delivered last week, only the names have been changed. The standards of excellence offered to families should be the same day in and day out. Same quality, same standards every time.

4. Tactfulness

A Funeral Celebrant must never share confidences about families or pass on information they have received at a family interview. This sounds so easy but you might be surprised about what gets shared. Celebrants cannot be gossips or worse still get caught saying things like, 'Oh do you know what this man died of...', or 'Oh you should have seen the state of the house I visited last week, it was...' Be discreet, be respectful.

The Funeral Directors Celebrants work with or the Chapel Attendant at the crematorium should not know details of any family. The day the Celebrant talks about someone is the day that comment will get back to the family and unsurprisingly, if they didn't like the comment, the Celebrant will soon hear about it.

5. Calmness

It goes without saying that many people need reassurance when you walk into a family home for the first time to conduct the family interview. What if the widow is extremely nervous and cannot talk for crying?

People like to be led and reassured at a funeral and know that you will look after them on the day. Tell the family at the end of the family interview that everything will be fine because you will make sure of it.

Even if you make a mistake during a service, stay calm. I have been heckled a couple of times, had mobile phones go off and even had Funeral Directors trying to pass messages to me during the service. All sorts of things can go wrong. I love the story of the church minister talking about the sun always shining on the righteous of this earth and at that exact moment the spotlight over his head popped and he was bathed in darkness. At one funeral I conducted, the curtains closed during the service when the family had asked for them not to be closed causing unnecessary anxiety.

Whatever has the potential to put you off your stride, stay calm because above everything the family want a reassuring presence. On another occasion I turned up at a graveside and the coffin would not fit into the grave. The widow was deeply distressed. I felt it was right to put my arm around her shoulder and take her for a little walk away from the grave until the situation was rectified. We all know that mistakes will happen and things will go wrong but at times like these people need their stress levels reduced not increased.

6. Politeness

People will annoy you and people may make mistakes. The Celebrants job is to be polite always and to maintain good working relationships. In this business it is not worth falling out with anyone. If necessary, accept responsibility, make an apology or eat a large slice of humble pie

The basic speaking skills of a Civil Funeral Celebrant

Try this one at your next public speaking engagement; "Fornication! Fornication! Fornication! ...For an occasion such as this as I am delighted to be here." I bet everyone will listen to you especially if you shout the words for-an-occasion.

In order to be an effective communicator, you need certain skills, a lot of practice and a good dose of humility. Modesty allows the Celebrant to see they can always improve their speaking skills and become a better communicator. To be an effective communicator at a funeral you need all of the standard public speaking skills and a wee drop more.

Speaking at a funeral is unlike any other form of public speaking, most notably because of the emotional attachment and the fact that the person who you are speaking about is no longer there, but his wife and children may be in the front row looking at you. It carries its own brand of anxiety. I conducted the funeral of a lady whose son was a well known actor in Scotland, another whose daughter is a well known celebrity. Both of these well known people spoke at the funeral and both broke down. It is a tough gig speaking at a funeral. I would say that in the above examples much of the anxiety relates to the fact that they intimately knew their audience and sometimes it doesn't take much to make you cry. Someone from your family may catch your eye at the wrong moment, or the particular story you are trying to recall about your dad could be the saddest moment of your life and it could be you – away, unable to speak. Some people can speak amazingly well at their parent's funeral or at the service of someone to whom they were really close, but not many. Most people would find this one of the hardest things to do.

Putting aside the challenges of speaking at a parent's funeral or speaking at a funeral for the first time (see Chapter 7), one of the first points to note about speaking at a funeral is that the audience or congregation in front of you have varying and different needs. Some people will deeply love the person whose funeral is being celebrated; others may only be present at the funeral for social reasons and to 'be seen'. Some may even dislike the person who lies in the coffin and may not have forgiven them for a past misdemeanour. I have even experienced the odd occasion where someone said to me, 'That was a lovely funeral you delivered there, but I am actually here for the next funeral. I arrived early, just sat down and decided just to stay anyway.' In other words, every audience you speak to is different.

Although your audience will have different needs and reasons for being at the funeral, your job is to create a sense of occasion and establish within those 20 or 30 minutes a relationship with your audience. A relationship which will enable people to not only hear what you have to say and understand your message but also feel the message through your passion, your sincerity and your ability to reach into their hearts and minds, not just their ears.

We cannot overlook the very basic fact that a funeral is a human event and our primary purpose, as speakers, is to ensure that our message will stimulate our audience's hearts and imaginations. You want to hear people tell you at the end of the funeral; 'You brought my father to life', 'You painted a marvellous picture of my brother', 'You did my father proud' or as Pam Vetter said in her foreword, the highest compliment can be, 'thank you...I heard every word'.

These are some of the greatest compliments you can receive as a speaker because they tell you, that not only was your message heard and understood but it was felt by the audience, they felt moved, and they felt that you had painted a picture that they recognised and appreciated.

From a human perspective we must never talk at people, we talk with them and for them. We aim to make the audience participants in an experience, not mere spectators at an event. A tip, this is probably one of my more important tips. When you speak at a funeral, avoid using the word 'you', use the inclusive 'we' instead. There are even occasions when I feel it is appropriate to say 'dad' instead of 'your dad'. Some Celebrants may feel uncomfortable about this and say, 'but I did not know the person, how can I talk about the love 'we' have for John when I am not a member of the family?' That is my point. You are speaking on the family's behalf, you are their advocate. Apart from that, the word 'you' is very impersonal while 'we' is inclusive. If you can confidently deliver a service as if you knew the individual, you have cracked one of the most important secrets of how to speak well at a funeral.

Ultimately, we are trying to take an audience 'with us'. This will depend on many factors including: how you are dressed, your body language, whether you give the impression you are 'reading' or not, how you communicate your message, eye contact and so forth. It is not just what is said by the Celebrant but how it is said. You are being asked to be a passionate speaker, to be an artist and a performer. You are 'on stage'. There must be a connection and a relationship between you and your audience and you should aim to have the audience feeling moved and touched to their core.

This type of delivery also demands a certain amount of giving of yourself in terms of emotional energy, empathy, sincerity and a belief that your words are feeding your audience, helping them get through this very difficult day and making the funeral celebration a heightened experience.

It also demands some basic voice techniques and it is these that we will be exploring in the following chapters. The use of pause, voice modulation, sliding words, speeding up and slowing down are important skills that a Celebrant and speaker must possess. You are trying to give an impression, like a painter, through your words, expressiveness and body language that you understand where this family are coming from and you will articulate the thoughts and feelings that are in their hearts.

Now isn't that a wonderful job and privilege? To speak on behalf of someone else and convey exactly what they feel and think; to move an audience and to interpret other people's thoughts and feelings. I have already mentioned the fact that a Celebrant may well receive a round of applause from a congregation but they may also been moved to tears. Every time I officiate at the funeral of a motor-biker and 20 motorbike engines rev up as the coffin arrives at the front of the crematorium all the hairs stand up on the back of my neck. I can feel my voice weaken and I genuinely feel moved by this biking tribute.

The privilege and challenge to be an effective communicator at a funeral is awesome. I can, within a 20-minute ceremony, touch people's hearts and strengthen their inner psychology. I know from experience that people do not want to be 'preached at' anymore. They want a funeral with a personal touch and to find the ceremony and the words that work best for them. Most of the people

I am communicating with are un-churched but this does not mean they don't have a soul and inner spiritual life that needs feeding. I aim to make real connections to people's hearts on the day of the funeral and for people to leave thinking that person was worth remembering. In effect I am bringing 'life' to the dead and giving them a legacy that will live on.

Chapter 5

Every Breath You Take – The Police

The art of being a memorable speaker at a funeral.

In this chapter I will offer you three practical steps to enable you to become an effective and hopefully brilliant communicator at a funeral. The first step relates to breathing, the second step offers six techniques to vary your voice and keep your audience interested and the third step is power of body language.

When I first started visiting Funeral Directors in the summer of 2005 in the hope of getting my first ever funeral, I literally knocked on the door of 40 Funeral Directors in Central Scotland and told them about this new and exciting profession that had come from Australia; the world of Civil Funerals.

Every Funeral Director except two was interested in what I had to say. I encountered genuine enthusiasm about the profession. At one point I was bold enough to predict that if Funeral Directors used the services of professionally trained and accredited Civil Celebrants, they would add value to their business and bottom line. The reason being, that families would be so impressed with the Civil Celebrant's professionalism that not only would they remember the Celebrant's name and recommend him or her to other bereaved family and friends, they would remember and recommend the name of the Funeral Directors who put them in touch with the Celebrant in the first place. I know this is the case from Customer Satisfaction Surveys I have carried out. Bereaved families often make comments to the Funeral Directors like, 'thank you for recommending Neil Dorward to us; he was worth his weight in gold'.

However, in these early days as much as I could talk the talk and walk the walk I still had to convince the first Funeral Director to hire me. When you are trying to sell yourself or your product, it is easy to tell them about what you do, you can even dig deep and tell them why you are doing this kind of work. The next stage is to convince them. People ultimately do not so much want to know about you as what you can do for them and their business. I had therefore to convince these Funeral Directors that I could make their lives better. My opportunity to convince them about what I could do for both the family and the Funeral Directors industry arose within one of my first funerals.

First impressions count

You can possibly imagine a Funeral Director's anxiety at unleashing someone whom they had never heard speak before. Their professional reputations as Funeral Directors were on the line with the family. If the person they hired turned out to be a disaster they might lose future business with that family, business that could take years to regain. Most Funeral Directors want the right person to fit the family's need but as I was the first person in Scotland to be a full time Civil Funeral Celebrant you could understand their temptation to default to people they had tried and tested already.

Imagine what might have gone through the minds of the Funeral Directors when they gave me one of my first opportunities. Unknown to them, the family had asked me to sing a song at the start of the funeral service. The man who had died used to be a local club entertainer and always began his Saturday night routine at the club where he was the MC with the song, 'The sun has got his hat on hip hip hip hurrah'. During the family interview the family asked me if I would be prepared to sing this song during the service. Picture the scene. The family step out of black funeral cars, slowly move into the crematorium chapel, the Funeral Directors reverentially place the coffin at the front of the crematorium whilst a piece of quiet reflective music was being played. The Funeral Directors then solemnly bow before the coffin in their black suits and walk out of the chapel in a respectful and dignified manner. Just as they exit the crematorium chapel and close the main doors behind them, I burst into song and the speaker system resounds, 'The sun has got his hat on hip hip hip hurrah'. Immediately Funeral Director's heads turn and have looks on their faces that say, 'What's going on here, who is this guy we have just hired?' They loved it and so too did the family.

I made a true connection that day with the Funeral Directors in terms of what I can do for them and made a connection with the family in giving them the best service they could have imagined. I also set the standards of excellence that every other Civil Funeral Celebrant who I subsequently trained would have to attain, if not exceed. A new profession had arrived in Scotland and the feedback from families and Funeral Directors was awesome, many telling me they had been waiting years for such a service to be provided and now they have an even greater portfolio of resources to offer their families.

Civil Celebrants in Scotland had arrived and for the next two years I single handedly flew the flag for the emerging profession and completed a one year diploma with the International College of Celebrancy in Australia.

Looking back on these first Civil Funerals in Central Scotland, it is clear that first impressions count. I had to create a spark. I felt I was setting the standard for how other Civil Celebrants would be judged. In all forms of communication, you only get one chance to make a first impression. From the message on my mobile phone to the images on my web site; the very first words and images that a family sees will speak volumes about the kind of service being offered. When I speak to the family for the first time on the phone, the family will make a judgement about me because of what I say to them. The tone and empathy of my voice is telling people they can trust me. When I visit them in their family home they will make assumptions about me and decide there and then if I am someone they can trust with one of the greatest treasures in their family – the legacy of their loved one.

A friend lost her mother a few years ago and what she told me has always stuck in my mind. She said the church Minister never offered his condolences to her or said a prayer when he visited her home. When I phone a family for the first time, I may not know them but it is common courtesy to say you are sorry to hear about their loss. They might quickly retort, "Oh it was a blessing, he had been suffering". But it is important to show some interest in someone who, in effect, is hiring your professional services. They will make judgements and assumptions about you by your voice, the way you dress, the way you shake their hands and what they see in your eyes.

The family interview is a one-off opportunity for the Celebrant to sell themself as someone who can be trusted. Imagine a stranger walking in to your home and asking you to open your heart, asking deep and sometimes intimate questions. In effect the Celebrant is inviting the family to say, 'Trust me, I will look after you, I will do you proud'. That same compassionate and warm person the family met in the living room and to whom they possibly poured out their hearts must be the same person the family meet on the day of the funeral. You cannot arrive late, you cannot forget the CD you said you would bring, you cannot stand there at the end of the funeral service and hand out your business card to other mourners in the hope of getting future business. Believe me it has happened!

Here is a family who have entrusted one of the most treasured and precious possessions they have in this world. The life story, the memory and the legacy of their loved one. They want to know you will talk about this person they loved as if you were a close family friend. Likewise, when they bump into you six months later in the fruit and veg aisle at Asda they want to meet the same person who came to their home six months previously.

You are the brand, you sell yourself

I believe I am in the business of communicating 24/7, communicating my standards, communicating what you will get every time you hire my services. But central to everything I do for a family and how I brand myself is how I speak on the day of the funeral. It sounds pretty straight forward to say all communication must be heard, understood and felt? But having witnessed dozens of other Celebrants and Ministers lead funeral services, I know this is not the case in Scotland. There was even an amazing case in Bellshill in Scotland of a distraught family putting an advert in their local paper apologising for the dreadful service delivered at a funeral. They were so disappointed about what was said that they issued a public apology in the newspaper.

It is possible for anyone to be a great funeral speaker but it will take hard work. Just because you speak at your work or have delivered a best man's speech does not mean you will be an effective communicator at a funeral. A funeral is a unique event and demands a certain style or speaking like no other.

I am going to show you how to be a great funeral speaker and offer you practical steps so that you will communicate with passion. If you aspire to inspire those who have come to a funeral to pay their respects, I will help you get there.

These are the very basics. In order for any communication to be heard, your breathing must be balanced, your voice must be clear and meaningful and your body language must be right. It is true to say that your voice is an instrument and like all instruments it needs to be practised. If you speak to any singer they will tell you about singing from the diaphragm not the throat. The same is true in public speaking. We should not speak from the throat and the head but from the diaphragm and the heart.

The voice must be clear and well projected, with no mumbling, and the meaning must be clear, crisp and articulate. You must convey meaning with every word and sound you make. People do not like mumbling and 'punch lines' that cannot be heard or understood.

The following three steps will help make you a more effective communicator at a funeral; breathing, clarity of words and body language.

Practical step one - *breathing*

Katherine Jenkins is not only beautiful to look at; she is beautiful to listen to. Like all trained singers she breaths from the stomach, well the diaphragm. It sounds so simple to say; you must take sufficient breath before you speak or your voice quality will not be good enough. However, we have to accept that we can all be affected by nerves and that most breathing problems within the public speaking arena are caused by anxiety. Sometimes, without warning, nerves can just overtake us and you have to know how to cope with that.

Consider the following scenarios and think about how you would cope.

1. You meet with the family to discuss the funeral. It is December and the family asks to sing 'Silent Night' during the funeral. You are unsure as to whether that hymn is in the crematorium hymn book, so you phone the crematorium office the day before the funeral and they confirm the hymn is in the hymn book. Great, you are relaxed, you turn up for the funeral the next day, everything is going well, you then announce it is time to sing the hymn and ask everyone to turn to hymn number 176 to sing Silent Night. Oh dear, within seconds you realise that the words printed in the hymn book are a totally different version of Silent Night that most people are familiar with and you do not therefore have the version of Silent Night that the family had specifically requested. What do you do?

   When this happened to me I simply announced that the words in the hymn book and the well known words of 'Silent Night' (that we all know) did not match up but we would try our best to sing the traditional version of the hymn because that is what Mary requested for her service. I also offered to lead the singing and tried to make light of a genuine error.

2. You have delivered an excellent tribute, the funeral has gone really well, you make the final announcement thanking people for their presence here today and you announce, 'Our service is ended let us go in peace and love'. Just at that moment, when you walk down from the pulpit, a member of the family unexpectedly and without warning announces that the service is not over as one of the grand children, an eight year

old girl with a crumpled piece of paper wishes to read two poems to her granddad. What do you do?

Although I was unaware that this eight year old girl had intended to read a poem, it was clear she wanted to do this. So I asked everyone to sit down again, she read her poems, we gave her a round of applause and then it was announced, 'This time ladies and gentleman, our service has ended, thank you'. All was well.

3. Just before the service begins, a member of the family hands you several pieces of paper, written in their almost illegible hand writing and asks you to deliver this tribute on their behalf. What do you do?

On the couple of occasions when this happened to me, I tried my best to read the notes 'on the spot'. If there is a point within the service when you can have a glance at the notes before you read them properly, such as during the singing of a hymn, then take that chance. Sometimes if the additional notes are lengthy there may not be time to read everything. I was speaking to a Minister recently about this scenario and when he was handed five sheets of hand written A4 paper from a grandchild, he let the congregation know it would not be possible to read every word but he was prepared to read the whole tribute later on at the hotel where they were going for refreshments.

All of these scenarios are enough to put you off your stride and affect your breathing. Most public speakers do not have major breathing difficulties during a public performance but now and again you can be thrown a 'swerve ball' that catches you off guard and it only takes one small incident for your anxiety levels to rise and your breathing to be adversely affected. You have to be prepared for all 'emergencies' but as a golden rule, always be calm and cool and look as if you are not flustered at all. At times you will be called upon to control your nerves and your breathing, normally when you least expect it.

I conducted a funeral where I saw someone in the congregation who I knew from many years ago in a working capacity. That person and myself never got on at work, he was a bit of a bully to me, and so I left my job and went somewhere else. I had not seen him in a long time and all of a sudden there he was half a dozen rows in front of me. Before I uttered my first words I was aware that my heart rate had increased, I felt very nervous seeing him again still smiling obnoxiously. Here I was about to speak and I could not control my breathing. I started the service but I felt my voice quiver and it took me a few paragraphs into the service before I relaxed. About a year later, the same person was there again at another funeral and this time I decided I was going to take control of my breathing and my thoughts. I had decided that if this scenario was to happen again I would, right at the beginning of the service, before I started speaking, smile inwardly and look that person in the eye and show him I was not anxious with his presence and it worked. Smiling is a great way to tackle breathing problems. A smile will relax you in more ways than one. The point to make here is that breathing/ heartbeat can be physically and consciously controlled. Indeed the old adage 'just take a deep breath' does work before you speak in public, as does an inner confidence that you will perform well. Good posture is another good habit to develop, literally standing tall (says the man who is five foot five and half) aids breathing. If you know the cause of the tension, then you have the remedy.

Practical step two – *keeping your audience interested by how you say the words*

The worst mistakes public speakers make are to talk too fast and mumble. The first can be mastered through breathing; the second can be mastered by simply opening your mouth. You may be surprised how many people mumble, half finish words, lack crispness and clarity and don't open their mouths sufficiently. The best way to find out if you mumble is to have yourself videoed or ask someone if you speak clearly. There is no excuse for mumbling. Make a conscious effort to open your mouth, slow down and really articulate the words, this should cure the mumbling.

Once you have the breathing and mumbling issues sorted, the next thing you must do is to introduce variation into your voice and vary the volume/loudness and softness, the up and down pitch where your voice goes high and low, by effectively using pause, small amounts of silence together with enunciation and clarity of words.

Words are powerful and within a funeral we have to understand that a single word and how it is delivered can potentially have a massive positive or negative effect. I was once asked to remove a sentence from a eulogy but mis-read the email and took out the wrong sentence. This meant that five words which should not have been said were said on the day and those few words were enough to upset one member of the family. Five small words are all it took. On another occasion I was going to introduce someone at the beginning of the service as 'partner' to the person who had died but with hours to go was told not to say the word partner and use the word 'friend' just in case someone from 'the social' (the DHSS) was in the congregation that day and it led to the DHSS starting some kind of investigation.

In addition to ensuring that the right words are said and the wrong words are not said there are other general rules to abide by. You should, for example, never over emphasise words and speak in an artificially loud manner as you may sound forceful or conceited. Don't speak like a salesman, as we are not in the business of selling. Neither should you be monotone or underplay words as you may sound dull and uninterested. Your voice projection should also be natural and unforced which will be the case if you are breathing properly.

In short there are six areas of voice tone that you should be aware of; pace, volume, pitch, enunciation/clarity, punctuation and pause.

1. PACE

You will be amazed at the impact your speech can have at a funeral simply by slowing down at certain parts of a sentence and speeding up on other parts. If you use the same pace and tone all the time you will put your audience to sleep but if you vary the speed of your words you will connect with your audience and emphasise what is important or not important.

Try reading this with your normal voice but slow down on the bold italics;

Think of me as one at rest, *for me you should not weep*
I have no pain no troubled thoughts for *I am just asleep*
The living *thinking me that was*, is now forever still
But life, life goes on without me now, as time forever will.

So your heart is heavy now because I've gone away
Dwell not long upon it friend; *For none of us can stay*
Those of you who liked me, *I sincerely thank you all*
And those of you who loved me, I thank you most of all.
And in my generous lifespan, as time went rushing by
I found some time to *hesitate, to laugh, to love, to cry*
Matters it not if time began; If time will ever cease
I was here... I used it all... and now... I am at peace.

2. VOLUME

I remember visiting a friend of mine at his teaching practice many years ago and I think he wanted to impress the children he was teaching. He was talking about the Big Bang Theory and without hyping up the topic to the pupils, he said something along the line of, 'OK everyone today we are going to look at the big [he said all these words at his normal speaking volume] BANG theory' – and roared the word 'bang' at the top of his voice. You could see some of the pupils jump a couple of inches off their chairs, they were genuinely startled. I was there too and I jumped when he said "BANG" at the top of his voice. But at least he got his message across, the variation in volume really worked for that particular sentence. I would bet to this day that many of the kids who went to that particular school will still remember that lesson.

When you speak in public it is essential to raise and lower your voice to maximise the impact of the message. You must have variation of volume or you will almost hypnotise your audience. Never offer to do a Burns Supper, for instance, if you cannae gan up an doon wi yir volume (if you can not go up and down with your volume). A Burns Supper is a traditional Scottish evening to celebrate the life and works of Robert Burns.

In this example, bold letters equate to an increase in volume, underlined letters to a reduction on volume and the remaining words are delivered at the same level.

> Is there for **honesty poverty**
> That **hings his head,** an' a' that;
> The coward slave <u>we pass him by,</u>
> We dare be <u>poor for a' that!</u>
> **For a' that, an' a' that,**
> Our toils obscure <u>an' a' that,</u>
> The **rank** is but the guinea's stamp,
> The man's the gowd for <u>a' that.</u>

3. PITCH

In addition to variation in volume, you must have variation in pitch at the end of each sentence. One of the students on my training course had been speaking for 20-plus years in the public sector and he didn't realise that the pitch of his voice went down on every sentence he spoke and what a major affect that had on the listeners' ears. It was very monotone and boring. If you have a chance, do a quick internet search for the famous John F Kennedy speech in 1961 when he said, 'Ask not what your country can do for you but what you can do for your country'. This is a great example of pitch, so too are some of Winston Churchill's speeches.

I offer you another tip. If you want to find some of the best speaking voices and the most interesting voices listen to radio adverts and take time to note how they really use their voices. Because we cannot see any images on the radio, the speakers have to make concerted efforts to paint pictures with their voices and ensure the advertising message is received, understood and felt. Celebrants must do the same. We must convey meaning with words and almost paint pictures with them just like a Marks and Spencers food advert that was shown on TV throughout 2008; this is not ordinary food, it claimed, this is Marks and Spencers food and viewers almost salivated with the words and pictures in that famous advert. The voice tones and variations in pitch aided the desire to go out and buy M&S food as pictures were painted with words.

4. ENUNCIATION/CLARITY

When I was in primary school I remember someone daring me to say, 'I saw a ship in sight' three times very fast and of course the third time I would have said, 'I shaw a ship in shite'. Believe it or not I got the belt for that in Primary 7 and never got the quarter ounce of cola cubes that I was promised for the dare. What was not so funny was seeing my 10-year-old friends grimace as the Lochgelly tawse (leather belt) marked my hands with this red V sign three times. Oh some teachers were incredibly cruel back then and belted you for almost no reason. The point to be made is that enunciation, diction and pronunciation are very important.

As public speakers we must, with every single sentence be asking ourselves, "How much feeling can I convey with this sentence? Am I convincing the audience that I believe and feel what I am saying?"

I mean, if you were speaking to a Funeral Director over the phone and were trying to ascertain the details for a funeral for which you do not have confirmed written details. You could possibly say the following sentence in three ways,

"Could you confirm the time of the funeral today?"

You could say that sentence in a polite manner to the Funeral Director and even smile while you say it. Or you could deliver that message in a grumpy manner because you have been waiting all day for this telephone call to be returned to you and you are a bit cheesed off that it hasn't come. Or you could communicate that sentence with a certain air of authority, maybe even arrogance, so that they will phone you back in the next five minutes or else.

In other words, it's the way you say it. All words do not hold the same value. At a funeral, we are not reading a book or a newspaper and from a public speaking perspective, we should not give words equal value.

For example, imagine these words being said, at the most poignant moment of a funeral service at a crematorium, when the curtains close.

John Smith

Your life we honour *(same tone)*

Your departure, we accept *(pitch and volume down on 'we accept')*

Your memory we cherish *(pitch and volume up the whole sentence)*

And although there is grief today at your death *(same tone)*

There is gratitude for your life *(pitch and volume up on 'gratitude')*

We are truly grateful for the privilege of having shared life with you

Rest at the end of your days *(slowing down on 'rest')*

Your work is done *(same tone)*

Rest in the hearts and minds of all who love you

And if we can learn from his experience *(pace increased, same tone)*

And profit from his example *(same pace as above but increase volume again)*

Perhaps we can live better lives for having known him *(upward pitch on 'him')*

What this example shows is that during one of the most crucial moments within the funeral service, the final farewell/the closing of the crematorium curtain, your words must be clear and have variation in volume and tone in order to denote empathy.

5. PUNC-TU-A-TION

This tip is so simple we often forget to use it. By punctuating a word we force ourselves to slow down, we encourage people to listen and that single word we are punctuating will have an impact on the listeners' ears. Repeat the phrase "I am an articulate speaker" in a normal voice without punctuating the word 'articulate', then repeat by punctuating this word 'ar-tic-u-late'. You can use this effect all the time, even the word 'punctuate' can be punc-tu-a-ted. All good speakers punctuate and accentuate certain words for impact value. This is an easy way to make an impact. If all you do is punctuate and vary your voice tone and nothing else you will make a big difference to the communicated message.

6. The PAUSE

There was a fantastic advert on the radio a few years ago with the words read by Bob Hoskins. He started off by saying these words; "It's ... (then there was a 3 second pause) ...it's (then there was a 2 second pause) it's... (a 1 second pause) ...it's frustrating isn't it when people don't talk?"

The impact of the pause was brilliant. The advert drew the listener in first through curiosity and then kept them hooked by sheer frustration. You can almost hear wee voices inside people's heads saying, "Get on with it Bob, you're driving me nuts... give me the message!"

The pause is one of the simplest and most effective tools we can use as a public speaker and it is vastly under used. Pause and silence are fantastic tools to use within a funeral service. One minute you can have your audience laughing with some story about the man who insisted on being buried with his favourite rock band T-shirt on. The band's name was 'Tool' and he reckoned he would be the first person in heaven with the word 'Tool' emblazoned on his chest. The next moment that same family could be moved to tears with stories of how their dad raised loads of money for charity while he was battling his brain tumour. In such a scenario you would deliver the T-shirt story in an interesting and engaging way then pause as you linked it to how brave he was fighting his cancer. Look for places within the ceremony where the pause will have its greatest effect.

In summary – In order to have meaningful and clear words your voice should have:

- Variation in pace (sometimes you speak fast, at other times you speak slowly)

- Variation in volume (soft emphasis and louder delivery when appropriate)

- Variation in tone (gliding of words)

- Good punctuation

- Good enunciation

- Use of pause

It is the constant variation of pace, tone and strength that will make your voice interesting. Above all, diction must be clear. The way we speak should be clear. There may be times when we have to focus on the shape of our mouth to ensure words are being clearly articulated. It is a good exercise every once in a while to accentuate the mouth, tongue, lips and jaw. Try it sometime when you are driving in the car, do some real vocal exercises and it will make a difference. If you want to make an even greater difference, sing in your car at the top of voice, sing your favourite song, like an athlete warming up those muscles and let a secret voice in your head say: "I am going to deliver an awesome performance today".

Vocal agility and clarity are the basic tools a Celebrant needs. In order for words to be meaningful and to have impact simply vary the speed, the modulation and the volume of your voice and add in the occasional pause and punctuation for additional effect.

As a Celebrant, your projection should be effortless and ultimately you should be able to think as you talk and almost read one sentence ahead of yourself. This would be one of my top tips to public speakers at a funeral. Do not read the text. You wrote the text, you know what is coming up in the next sentence, you should be able to look down and memorise a couple of sentences at a time and deliver them whilst looking up and making eye contact with the family. Speak to the hearts of the family as if they are the only people in the room. Make a connection, that is the only thing you must do, convince people that your message is important and it must be listened to. If you can do this you will be a huge success as the element of trust that you established on the very first telephone call, built up at the family interview and with the telephone call to the family the night before the funeral, will now come to fruition. I have had many people tell me afterwards that I kept them going and that how I spoke to them during the service gave them strength and peace.

Often we are communicating to the hearts of the grieving and broken and they want to see from the way you read the script that you feel their pain, are with them on this journey and understand where they are coming from. Yes there is a risk in this approach. To this day many people remember the former Prime Minister Tony Blair 'Queen of our hearts' speech when Princess Diana died and some people, in later years, criticised him for being insincere. I think this criticism is unjust because as much as we can look back on that speech and think there is an element of fakery and acting, on the day, it worked. It worked on the day because everyone was touched by Princess Diana's death and he was simply reflecting the mood of the nation at that precise moment.

It is true that on most occasions I have never met the person who has died and yet I am charged with speaking about them as if I knew them. I am like the advocate for the family. I am doing something they ideally would like to do but cannot. This is not conning people, it's providing a wonderful service and I feel the Celebrant must put a certain level of emotion, warmth and sincerity into their words. I don't think this is duping people at all, it is simply offering comfort to the bereaved and speaking well of the dead. Since most folk, including myself, would find it difficult to speak at a funeral of a mother or father, the next best thing is a professional speaker and Celebrant. That is our job, to bring the dead to life, to speak well of them and to be the advocate of the family on this most special of days.

Remember too that there are different forms of literature. We do not read a love poem to our wife on a wedding anniversary the way you would read a newspaper. Similarly within the funeral service the opening words, the poem, the eulogy, the words spoken at the committal and the announcements at the end to invite people to have a cup of tea and a bun should all vary. In other words, a well constructed funeral service has an in-built structure that aids variation in voice. It is not just what is said but how it is said that makes the difference. That is why it is almost impossible to 'copy' someone else's funeral script and pass it off as your own.

Try reading this with variation of volume, pitch and tone

The Alternative Beatitudes (author Unknown)

Blessed are those who can laugh at themselves,
they will have no end of fun

Blessed are those who can tell a mountain from a molehill,
they will be saved a lot of bother

Blessed are those who know how to relax without looking for excuses,
they are on the way to becoming wise

Blessed are those who know when to be quiet and listen,
they will learn a lot of new things

Blessed are those who are sane enough not to take themselves too seriously,
they will be valued by those about them

Blessed are you if you can take small things seriously and face serious things calmly, you will go far in life

Blessed are you if you can appreciate a smile and forget a frown,
you will walk on the sunny side of the street

Blessed are you if you can be kind in understanding the attitudes of others,
you may be taken for a fool but this is the price of charity

Blessed are you if you know when to hold your tongue and smile,
kindness has begun to seep into your heart

Blessed are they, who think before acting and pause before thinking,
they will avoid many blunders

Blessed are those who recognise goodness in all who they meet,
the light of truth shines in their lives. They have found wisdom.

Blessed are those who dream dreams
but are ready to pay the price to make them come true

Practical step three – *body language*

This third step is again so important. The way we stand or fold our arms, the way we move our eyes, the way we flick our hair, it is all part of how we communicate. Non verbal communication speaks volumes. We do it every day. Your wife or girlfriend colours her hair and she asks you, after it was all styled and blow dried, 'What do you think darling?' Now this man (let's call him Neil) physically sees no difference whatsoever between his wife's hair at the dinner table than what he saw in the morning, he might even think he prefers the hair style he saw eight hours ago. 'Oh yeh', he says, 'your hair looks great'. It's just words; you don't have to mean them. It's easier to tell a small white lie and make someone feel good than say, 'Honey it's a mess'. But what was my body saying? Perhaps the comment Neil's wife says to him, 'Well you could at least look up from your computer screen' says it all. After a quick two-second look, she is told she looks great, but Neil's body language as he sits unmoved on his chair staring at his computer screen says something different along the lines: 'please leave me alone I'm busy'.

Body language is a major part of the communication message. Psychologists will say that the 'person' speaking the truth is your body.

Over my many years of working with the bereaved I know of the importance of body language. When I am visiting a family in their home, eye contact and how I position my body is so important. I communicate as much with my eyes and body as I do with my mouth. The first thing I do when I enter a family home to conduct an interview is to shake everyone's hands, say 'yes' to a cup of tea if offered and then position myself on a chair so that my body looks interested and engaged with what they are about to tell me. I am not there to sit back and be relaxed; I find it much better to sit almost on the edge of the seat so that I can move my body easily towards the person I am speaking to. Being on the edge of the seat also allows me to move my body inwards and towards the person from time-to-time and demonstrate an even greater degree of interest.

I am simply trying to establish a relationship of trust within minutes and from the thank you cards I receive from families I know they appreciate this sincere and relaxed approach. I am there to get information, to write someone's life story within an hour or two and I want people to talk and trust me. Body language plays a massive role here.

Now once that relationship of trust is established I will finish the interview by telling the family that they will have a draft copy of the service with them by that evening or the following morning, that they are in charge of this draft version of the service and can add, delete or change any words. I reassure them that I will speak well of their loved one on the day. Another building block to the trust equation is added. Hopefully this level of trust continues when they read what has been written and when I phone them up the night before the funeral and again tell them 'I am thinking of you'. The next day, as I greet them at the front door of the crematorium, perhaps with a smile or a handshake I remind myself that I am not the most important person at the funeral service. If the family step out of the funeral cars and look totally distraught, they may not want my hand extended towards them as they walk into the crematorium chapel, no matter how well intentioned it is. Be aware, try and read people's body language. I then deliver the service with the greatest passion and sincerity I can muster.

I always make a conscious effort not to 'read' the script but to communicate to the family with my eyes and from my heart. As already mentioned, I memorise a few lines at a time and try to speak the words directly to the family. The effect here, in my opinion, is very powerful. By using my eyes and body to communicate the message I generate a connection with the family who I have known for the last five days and who have trusted me to give them the best funeral service ever.

In order for this to happen I have to believe and feel what I have written. If during the family interview I am told that John was the best dad in the world (even though he possibly wasn't) then I have to believe the family and communicate this message. My task is to paint the 'true' picture of John as the family see it. My job is to bring life to the words and feel them. So, again, if John was an extremely funny man and the family ask me to re-tell a few funny stories from his life, I make sure that I re-tell these stories in an amusing or funny way, with a smile and body language that allows people to laugh and smile. Don't tell a funny story and impersonate a plank of wood, use effective body language. Re-tell the story almost as if you were with a group of John's friends in the pub when he put his false teeth in someone else's pint and they drunk it. Convince the audience and deliver both words and feelings. It is like those people who deliver great jokes badly- no one laughs. Look at comedians like Billy Connolly and Frank Carson; it is all about the delivery and convincing the audience that the story really is funny.

Ask any man or woman who speaks at Burns Suppers and they will tell you that they have studied the poem(s) they will be reciting that evening and they know what the words mean and how they should be delivered. They will know what facial expression and body language should be used to bring Burns words to life. The most effective speakers communicate with their whole body (smiles, eye contact, hand movements) and communicate empathy whilst telling the immediate family they are honouring that person's memory.

People may remember what you say but more important than that, people will always remember how they feel. Equally, if you miss the point, mumble, look disinterested in what you are saying or read from the script, people will talk about you for years to come as well; but sadly for the wrong reasons.

Imagine you are recalling some great story at a funeral and you plan to deliver the lines to an immediate member of the family, the widow for example, and as you speak, she catches your eye during the service. At that precise moment when your eyes catches hers there is a 'communication' between you, maybe even a smile, a smile that says to you, "this is right, this is true, this is what I want people to know about the person I love." Wouldn't you want the family to have that confidence and trust in you?

In other words as you deliver a tribute, read a poem, tell a funny story or recall an incident from someone's life you must bring that experience back to life for your audience through your words and your body language, otherwise you are as well photocopying the tribute, giving everyone a copy and asking them to read it for themselves.

Your audience is only interested in what they see, hear and feel and it must be brilliant each and every time. They want a ceremony that gives a heightened sense of occasion, they want a performance. When there is real communication on the same level, you have created a truly memorable ceremony for that family. You want your words, your body, and your eyes to have touched their soul. I would also encourage Celebrants to share some degree of personal emotion or at least give the impression you understand their loss. Make people feel something of your words.

I cannot put it simpler than this – do not 'read' the script. At the very least you must not give the impression that you are reading a script. Read the script several times before you deliver it, 'move away' from the written text and generate greater eye contact. Develop the skill to almost read one sentence ahead of you and know what is coming next.

Why not develop the confidence to ad lib slightly? In other words if you have to re-tell a good story try and memorise it. Let's say it is a short simple story about John going out in his boat one day with his best suit and jacket on and he accidentally slips, falls into the water and comes out with a salmon in his pocket. How long does it take to memorise that story and once it is memorised, tell it naturally? I guarantee that it will not come over to the congregation as being read and if you do this even half a dozen times in the tribute it will have a massive impact on how well your communication will be received.

I employ this technique of memorising and moving away from the script on a daily basis because it frees me to make greater eye contact with the immediate family and give the impression that I am with them on a familiar and intimate level.

People want you to look at them, it enhances communication. It will also enhance your own confidence as you receive communication back from your audience, such as a laugh, a smile or, sometimes a round of applause.

All Celebrants and public speakers should accept the fact that they will continue to learn about the art of communication. I would recommend all Celebrants to have themselves filmed. From that they will be able to identify what aspects of their body language need to be improved. It may be their posture, perhaps they need to stand up straight and tall and look authoritive. The video may tell them they move too much in the pulpit, sway from side to side or twiddle with their hands too much.

Alternatively ask someone you trust what they think of you and how you could improve your communication or at least remove the things that are distracting from the communication. The communication should move your audience and your body language and eyes should convey a message that says: this man or woman who you have come here today to pay your respects to deserves to be well spoken of and you should be glad to have known him and loved him. You are the lucky ones to have known and loved this person.

Being able to meet and exceed your audience's expectations is an art form that demands pastoral sensitivity and regular review of your public speaking skills since every public speaking occasion has different values and expectations to be met. The Australian public speaking coach E Jane Day reminds Celebrants that they can make or break a family's psychological state during a public service and that if delivered in a first class way can 'contribute to beauty and stability in society'. However, as all good voice coaches will remind you, Celebrants should be under no illusion that this demands work and interpretative skills. Being able to connect to people through words and to meet your audiences' hearts, minds, thoughts and feelings necessitates that you spend time developing your public speaking skills. It is all about serving families and when we know that is a privilege we will want to be the best.

Chapter 6

What Becomes Of The Broken Hearted – Jimmy Ruffin

The more challenging funeral ceremonies – Babies and children, murders and suicide.

When I was about age 10, I remember my mother discovering her favourite statue had been broken; the sellotape around the lady's head did not fool my mum. The statue of a beautiful lady was fixed but still to this day you can see where it was broken. The lines, the scars are still visible.

A broken heart will always have a scar. Any family who has suffered the agonising loss of a baby or child or has been bereaved through murder or suicide will be scarred and words very often will never be able to describe that pain. That scar may heal and disappear but it will never go away and the people left behind will cope in varying ways.

I will not pretend it is easy to speak at a funeral of a baby or child, or that it is easy to find the right words for a mum whose son was brutally murdered, or a family who are left with unanswered questions when someone they love takes their own life. Sometimes these kinds of funerals call for less to be said.

Babies and Children

Often when I visit a couple who have lost a baby or a child, I will honestly admit to them that I have no words of comfort for them but I wish I had. No matter how well intentioned we feel or how empathetic we are, often there are no words to take away the hurt and pain of losing a baby or child. As much as I may be moved at a funeral every time I see a white teddy bear coffin being lowered into the ground and rose petals gently landing on top of the coffin, I will never know what they are going through as parents. All I can do is be there for them and offer some words of comfort to them on the day of the funeral. Invariably that is all parents want, a short service, nothing that will prolong the agony.

Unlike a standard family interview where I might interview a family for a couple of hours and try and get as much biographical information as possible, this is not appropriate for a baby funeral or the funeral of a child. I find that the best way to approach these ceremonies is to offer the family a collection of poems and readings that would be appropriate for a baby or child funeral, and send them two or three sample copies of funeral services that I have already conducted, provided all the names and dates have been taken out. I know that point has been made already, that a Celebrant must never use the same script twice and be tempted to substitute names from one service to another but what I am referring to here is slightly different. I am encouraging the families to partially write the service themselves by looking at what other parents have put together for their babies and children. If parents can see what other mums and dads have done, it puts them in charge of the service. In other words give them a basic structure, write up a draft version of the service, give them further samples and then allow the family to change the draft according to their personal needs and wants. Some may want religious content others won't. Some may want music while others would find that inappropriate for them. Some parents want to express a hope that they will meet their baby or child again one day others may find that too personal and painful and not something they wish to share on the day of the funeral. Although the words said at a baby or child's funeral should be carefully chosen, involve the parents and family right from the start.

No-one ever expects to bury a child, but it can be appropriate for parents to talk about their dreams and hopes for their baby or child. But it is not appropriate to use humour or to talk about the baby or child being in a better place. Basically avoid any language that can lead parents to feel guilty or that they are to blame. Instead use the child's name as often as possible, talk of other people in the family like sisters, brothers, grandparents and so forth. If it is the parents' wishes, speak of the joy and happiness they may have felt before the birth or the happiness they shared in their child's short life and the love they will always have for their child. Again, if appropriate, talk about how difficult it is to embrace sorrow but always talk about the love the family had for that baby or child.

Analogies can sometimes help the family. I love the story of the gardener who could not understand why the rose in his garden did not grow this spring. All of his life he had seen beautiful roses bloom and flourish at their allotted time until one year, a single rose did not appear. No one can explain why this object of beauty did not show its full life this side of the earth.

From a speaking perspective, I would suggest that your voice tone and intimation should be slightly more subdued. Normally I would encourage all speakers at a funeral to show their artistry and their skills as an orator but during the funeral of a baby or child, the grief is so intense that your words are almost of little or no significance compared to what the family have to go through on that day. Similarly don't expect people to tell you what a lovely service that was. Simply be compassionate and understanding and remember that sometimes a lot of words don't need to be said.

Murder and manslaughter

There is no need to go into the legal definitions at this point, but such deaths are crushing, overwhelming and bewildering. As many support organisations will tell you, death of this kind can cause deep shock and agony not to mention feelings of anger and maybe even revenge.

I have conducted several services for those bereaved through murder and manslaughter and, from a ceremonial point of view, I have often found that the family's feelings and thoughts towards the perpetrator of the crime tend to be put to one side on the day of the funeral. It is as if the family are saying their lives have been in so much turmoil and grief in these last few days that they are determined to have as normal a funeral as possible. In all the instances where I have had to prepare a funeral service for a family bereaved by murder or manslaughter the general aim was not to let the cause of death drastically affect how they felt about their son, daughter, mother or father. There seems to be an understandable need to have a service for that person as if they had died of natural causes. Very often the brutality and violence of the death will not be mentioned although in one case it was and I was explicitly asked to talk about the evil people who had committed this crime.

I believe this approach of letting the family have as normal a service as possible helps them find some relief in what will have been an excruciatingly painful week. They may have already been under the scrutiny of the public eye but the funeral is theirs and is one of the few moments during this extremely difficult time when they are in charge of their loved one's life. The service is an opportunity for the family to have some kind of normality. This seems to be one area that no one can take away from them, an occasion to talk not so much about how (s)he died but how (s)he lived.

During these funerals the Celebrant can do his or her standard service of excellence but there is always an element of caution not to go too overboard with the idea of celebrating someone's life with inappropriate humour. This is a unique kind of mourning and the Celebrant again has to find the right words. There normally will be some acknowledgement of the immense sadness of this day but most families want the service to be as 'normal' as possible and they want to use it as a small stepping stone within the healing process.

The Celebrant should also be aware that there may be Police presence at the funeral and there may be Press interest but don't let this distract you from doing your very best for the family.

Suicide

"Suicide is painless" so goes the theme tune from the TV series M.A.S.H., but it's not true. For those affected by suicide there is a lot of pain. Death through suicide will trigger intense grief and mourning for family and friends left behind. All sorts of feelings will emerge: shock, guilt, social isolation and asking yourself 'Why?' Sadly many families will never know why and this can create even more stress within a family, especially when no-one is to blame. The truth of the matter is that often those left behind will never know the reason why someone took their own life and this can make bereavement even more difficult. One of the first reactions concerns the 'what ifs' and the 'if onlys'. 'What if I could have done more?', 'What would have happened if he had come and talked to us?' Suicide can even lead to close family and friends feeling more vulnerable themselves. We've not even touched upon the media attention yet; despite what M.A.S.H. says suicide is far from painless.

The approach I would recommend for a Celebrant is the same as for those bereaved by murder and manslaughter. Families of those who have taken their own life will use the funeral as a way of moving forward and as a way to mourn and let go. They want some kind of normality. Although the funeral day may not be the time or place to tell the immediate family there is life before suicide and after it, it may be appropriate to talk about the fact that no one is to blame and no one should feel guilty, or as I have sometimes said, 'John was not a coward for what he did'. There may be anger, there may be blame but most of the funerals I have conducted for those bereaved by suicide want a service that talks of the good and the happy times. There can be an acknowledgement that the individual had some hard times but the overall theme is one of remembering the better moments and just praying for their peace. For some families there may even be a sense of relief that their suffering is no more.

If during the family interview there are tears, remind the family that it is ok to cry. Tears release the flood of sorrow, of missing and of love. Tears can be healing. We do not need to 'prove' we loved someone and neither is guilt an indication that we love less. It means that, although we don't like what that individual has done we can learn to accept their choices in life. Similarly, if a family want to laugh and share funny stories, do that. Laughter is not a sign of 'less' grief or 'less' love it is a sign that many of our thoughts and memories are happy ones. It's a sign that we know our memories are happy ones. It's a sign that we know our loved one would want us to laugh again. It's ok to laugh.

Suicide causes a lot of pain for those left behind because people now know one of the most intimate secrets of that person's life, namely that they took their own life. We all have secrets that we would rather not be told at our funeral, but here we are in the full knowledge of what someone has done with their life and this can affect the way we might have thought about that person. A common reaction being 'I would never have imagined...' There is therefore a role for the Celebrant to realign the character of the individual and ensure his/her truest nature is celebrated on the day and people do not leave with a distorted impression of who they were. It is healthy to be honest at funerals of those who have taken their lives, but above all their love, goodness and decency must be respected, even if the decision they made for themselves is still painful to accept.

Suicide has traditionally been a taboo topic in western society, which has led to further alienation and only making the problem worse. We could go a long way to helping those bereaved by suicide by allowing them to have the exact service they want and even if that meant someone asking for that M.A.S.H. theme song to be played at the funeral, then so be it. If that particular song helps the broken-hearted let them have it. If a family don't want to be reminded of the bad times of their son's depression or schizophrenia, then stick to talking about the funny times and the laughs if that is what helps heal a family on the day of the funeral. You may never know what they are really feeling but if that is what the family need then give them that service.

As I said you might never know the family's real feelings. I once led a funeral for a family who had lost two children through suicide and at the end of the service I was walking back through the graveyard with someone who had come to pay their respects. I decided to make conversation with this individual. I made a comment along the lines of how difficult it must be to have lost two children through suicide and she cried and said, 'I have lost three'. You just never know. I have also conducted funerals for families where a very distressing and painful suicide note was left behind and far from healing the situation just made it a hundred times worse because certain people were named in the letter as the reason for the person taking their own life.

Be as positive and as uplifting as you can with these services. Remind the family of deep truths such as; "perhaps John never knew just how much he was loved and how much he is going to be missed", or, "although people die, the love we have for them does not."

In all of these services the voice tone of the Celebrant and your body language is vitally important as it will set the right mood and can help the family begin the healing process. The Celebrant has to be able to tap into exactly what the family want to be said and deliver the words in the right way. But remember the service is not about you, it's about them.

Chapter 7

I Can See Clearly Now – Jimmy Cliff

Advice to Celebrants in helping family members deliver a eulogy.

If during a family interview sometime tells you they want to speak at the funeral or it is the first time they have been asked to prepare a eulogy, you may be called upon to help and advise that individual.

As a Celebrant it is worth reminding ourselves that advice on how to write a eulogy would be dependent upon such things as,

- How close the individual was to the person who died?

- How the individual was connected to the deceased, was it through family, work, hobbies?

- Is there any, what you might call 'unfinished business' with the deceased, such as words said in the past that someone now regrets?

- Was the death expected or sudden?

- Was it easy to understand why the person died, as the cause may be unknown or the true nature of the death may be kept secret?

- The level of grief will be further affected if we are dealing with the death of a child, or suicide or murder.

My first bit of advice to anyone being asked to deliver a eulogy at a funeral would be to turn up.

I know that sounds very cheeky but it has happened to me several times. Granted, on most of these occasions, the person was in the congregation, they just took last-minute nerves and decided not to speak after all; that's perfectly ok. The other occasion, to be fair, was just a very close shave when someone turned up to deliver their tribute and forgot their notes. There was no way the lady could go back home for them or ask someone to deliver them as she had flown in from Holland that very day. It wasn't looking good given the fact that she arrived at the crematorium with the funeral about to start in a couple of minutes. This lady was clearly in a desperate panic, almost manic, wondering what she could do. It was like a last act of desperation as she waved this small red computer memory stick in front of me.

Although the funeral started just about on time, it was an interesting sight watching her fire up my laptop as she sat in the crematorium listening to the opening music and opening words of welcome. How fortunate I had my laptop in my car that day. I dare say it is not every day that a congregation will hear the all too familiar Microsoft Windows sound as the computer loaded but it was no worse than a mobile phone. The timing was very tight. Between the opening words and the reading of the poem she probably had four or five minutes to upload her file. Thankfully she found her script on the memory stick and boldly came to the lectern, laptop in hand, and delivered the eulogy to her gran flawlessly, and all before the battery packed up. What a feat. That lady was in fact one of best speakers I have ever heard at a funeral and spoke with deep passion and love about her gran.

That young woman who spoke at her gran's funeral showed remarkable courage, skills and determination to deliver her tribute, which brings me to the next point. If you decide to deliver a eulogy and change your mind at the last minute, don't worry, the Celebrant will cope. Likewise if you get half way through the tribute and cannot finish that's ok too. If you cry, you know what, people will still respect you.

If you have been asked to deliver a eulogy at a funeral and are worried about any of these scenarios occurring, feel free to ask someone in advance to step in for you. Just give them a copy of your eulogy in advance so they have a chance to read it. If you feel really nervous, bring someone up to the lectern to stand next to you. You will be amazed by the strength that can be drawn from that alone, of having someone physically stand next to you.

I make this point about "tips for first timers". There are lots of web sites out there that will offer you advice, but please remember that is all it is – advice. Please take it or leave it. I have come across many voices and bloggers out there who offer advice on to how to speak at a funeral. I read the blog of someone who said first timers must never look at people they know in the audience as this might put them off their stride. My advice would be the exact opposite. I would, from personal experience of speaking at hundreds of funerals, encourage anyone who was nervous in this situation to make a deliberate and concerted effort to look that person straight in the eyes to banish the nerves. The point I am trying to make here is that at the end of the day everything you read in this book or elsewhere is just advice. Take it or leave it. Better still, take the advice of everyone who makes sense to you and ignore the other stuff. Although to be fair to that social commentator, I did like her tip to first timers about relaxing after the service with a drink, a bath, a movie or whatever it takes to make you chill.

This being said, I would encourage all first timers to employ all the vocal tips in Chapter 5 and then select any of the following tips that resonate with you:

- Don't feel a need to introduce yourself at the beginning of your eulogy, and say, 'My name is Neil Dorward I am John's brother'. Most people will probably know who you are and remember too, you are not the important one, the deceased is. I know some guides say you should introduce yourself and explain your relationship with the deceased but let me make the point again: the family are the focus. Further, your name may already be printed on the Order of Service sheet, so there is no need to tell the congregation who you are.

- Speak about good and happy memories from the deceased life and if you are going to mention someone's failings, do so in a light hearted, tongue-in-cheek way: 'Aye Uncle George was a funny old sod especially when he did x, y and z'. Never use the eulogy to make a cheap shot; you'll look like a fool. Be respectful. One further tip, don't pick out quotes from dusty old books lying on a shelf or make references to John Keats and Oscar Wilde just to look well read and intelligent. Trust me, you won't.

- Avoid being over emotional and sentimental just for the sake of it. Don't hype up someone's illness or their last few hours on this earth. Don't do anything that will detract from the deceased and their family or plan, for example, to wrap your arms around the coffin and sob uncontrollably. Don't set out to make people cry, be respectful.

- Be yourself. If that means you want to wear a bright coloured shirt do so, if that means being funny because you are naturally funny then do so. Again, I have heard some people say don't wear casual clothes, don't stand out from the crowd. Yes don't, don't wear loud clothes just for the sake of it or try to be funny just for the sake of it. It only brings un-necessary attention to yourself. If, on the other hand, you always dress as a Goth or always wear a kilt to a funeral, do it, if that's who you are.

- If you think your eulogy will last four minutes, plan for eight. You will be surprised how fast the time goes unless you read at 100mph but that's a no-no as well. Many people tell me they have read their eulogy and have practised it many times and they know it will only take four minutes to deliver. The chances are, they read it in the quietness of their living room. Believe me; reading a bit of paper in the privacy of your own home is not the same as speaking in public. As a general rule double your time.

- Don't 'wing it' and just speak whatever comes into your mind or deliver a tribute without any notes. Yes, by all means ad lib, but please write everything down. If nothing else, in theory, someone else can take over if you decide you cannot finish the eulogy (although this is quite rare). Don't wing it and hope that the right words will come on the day. For a start you will waffle and lose track of time. In addition to that you run the risk of upsetting the next family who are waiting to come into the crematorium for their service by running over time. I have only seen three or four people come up and wing it. One person was brilliant but the other three definitely came over as poor speakers, unprepared and gave the impression that the few off the cuff remarks they came up with were all this chap deserves. A eulogy is a one off occasion, a one off opportunity to really speak well of the dead and remind people why they were so special. Write down every word of your script even if you plan not to 'read' the script or want to ad lib and create more of a conversational tone. Writing the eulogy down is just a safety mechanism that reduces unnecessary anxiety and acts as a back-up.

- Speak clearly and S-L-O-W-L-Y and try to start with a good opening line and end with an even better one. I cannot emphasise enough the importance of speaking slowly because your words will have greater impact. The same with having a good opening line. I heard one recently when someone said, 'My dad's life was never a travesty it was a tapestry' and a great finishing punch line when someone said, "send us a postcard card dad but please don't say 'Wish You Were here', at least give us a chance to enjoy the inheritance money."

- Speak from the heart not the throat and, if you can, look up and smile every now and again.

- Practice, Practice and Practice, that's three times but make it four with one of these being in front of the mirror.

- Look up at people not down at your notes, do not read or give the impression that your are reading your script.

- You are there to command 'the stage' and to touch people's hearts so make sure the content is relevant, informative, accurate, moving and if appropriate entertaining.

- I spoke about humour on pages 44-45 and how some people offer advice by saying 'you must make them laugh'. That's not the case. Use humour if it fits their personality, not yours. The first line of reference as to whether humour should be used in a funeral is the deceased's personality not yours. Be witty yes, be creative in your writing, be light hearted, but there is no compulsion to make 'em laugh. Do not use humour just for the sake of it or if the context is not there.

- If you make a mistake at any time, don't worry, most people will not notice. At a funeral recently, someone came up to me and said 'Isie didn't meet Jim at the dockyards you know, it was at the dancing'. No-one in the immediately family knew that. None of the three children knew where their mum and dad met and it was only as the family were leaving the crematorium that someone pointed this out.

- Do not deliver the eulogy in the Queen's English. When you speak at a funeral try the conversational approach - it is much friendlier and sounds warm, more authentic and paints a more realistic picture of the person you are speaking about.

I often tell individuals speakers not to write too much because what they think will take five minutes to read will take longer due to what I call emotional pauses. There are times my heart sinks when an additional speaker tells a family they will speak for five minutes and proceeds to bring five sheets of A5 paper from their inside pocket and the tribute seems to last forever.

I would further advise all families who use additional speakers to see a copy of their script in advance just in case there is something in it you would not approve of. On one such occasion, a speech was badly received by a family when stories were told about someone's previous girlfriend and names were mentioned inappropriately. Such stories are acceptable at a wedding where the aim may be to entertain but this is not the over-riding purpose of a funeral eulogy. I believe that such acts also put the focus of attention on the person delivering the eulogy rather than the deceased. A funeral is not the time or place to say to people; "hey look how funny I am". There was also the well known incident in the UK when the horse racing personality John McCririck spoke at the funeral of Robin Cook MP and Mr McCririck thought it appropriate to make a cheap remark at the then serving Prime Minister Tony Blair. That was wrong.

The Civil Funeral Celebrant is the servant and advocate of a family for the period for which he or she is hired. The family generally know what is best for them even if what you are asked to say doesn't meet with everyone's approval, c'est la vie. I can recall several funerals where I have explicitly been told by a family not to mention a certain person's name. It may be an ex-wife or husband

and then the brother of that ex-wife or husband comes to the funeral, sees that someone in his family has been completely written out of history and they might tell you, the Celebrant, that what you said or didn't say was wrong and unacceptable. Take it on the chin. Your job is to carry out the family's wishes.

Above all, remind all first timers to have confidence in who they are and their message and, of course, to speak from their heart. It is so important that all those who speak at funerals believe in themselves and deliver the communication with enthusiasm and conviction. We apparently have 60,000 thoughts a day, surely some of these thoughts can be along the lines of, 'My words will touch the hearts and souls of these people today' and 'I will give this family the very best service that I can deliver'. Of course confidence comes from practice and by having something worthwhile to say, but it's also an inner quality. If speakers are self confident, they are halfway there.

Chapter 8

It's My Party And I'll Cry If I Want To – Lesley Gore

Encouraging people to write their own eulogy.

You will come across individuals who want to take charge of their funeral service and either want you to write up their funeral service in advance or they want to write their own eulogy for you to deliver on their funeral day. Such people are absolutely right, the funeral is their party. Don't take that literally, but it is their funeral. They can do anything they want, in theory. I heard a lovely story of a man who owned an ice cream shop and everyone got a free tub of ice cream at the end of his funeral service.

In order to have the best possible funeral I would encourage all people to do two things:

1. Write some kind of eulogy or legacy statement in advance

2. Nominate the person who you want to speak at your funeral

In December 2008, a story ran in a newspaper in Northern Ireland about a man, who in all seriousness, celebrates Christmas every day of his life. He has presents every day, turkey every day and the Christmas decorations and the Christmas music is on 365 days a year. What is even more unusual about Andy Park is that he has now written down how he would like his funeral to be. His coffin will be carried by elves, the mourners must come dressed in Santa outfits, a few Slade Christmas songs will be played and, you can probably guess what all the mourners will be eating at the hotel reception afterwards.

Is this man crackers? Perhaps, perhaps not, but at least he has let his nearest and dearest know what he wants. He has let his family and friends know in advance how he would like to be remembered. He has taken control of what is arguably the most important day of his life. Most people do not plan what will be said and who will do the talking at their funeral but this is a scenario Celebrants will come across.

To write your own eulogy you may want to use the following guide:

- Detail your childhood, teenage years and adulthood by highlighting interests, hobbies, jobs, family, special memories etc.

- Try and share your values, beliefs and life's lessons

- Express appreciation to those who significantly shaped your life or brought you special joy, pleasure etc.

- Reflect on love, regrets, forgiveness/reconciliation (if applicable)

- Write your biography as a story. Tell the key parts of it; who you are, how you lived, who you loved, what you want people to know or understand about you, trying as much as possible to tell your life as you saw it

- Ask yourself , "What am I proud of?" or

- What am I most grateful for?

And hey presto! In addition to detailing your life the password to your computer has been revealed, permission has been granted to delete your browser history and hopefully you have nominated the person you want to lead the service (Minister, Priest, Civil Celebrant) and anyone else who will deliver a eulogy.

Write it down. Write your own eulogy and give some guidance to your family and friends as to how you would like to be remembered and what you would like your legacy to be. If you are really brave repeat this eulogy writing exercise by asking someone else to write their version of your life.

I love the idea that our lives should be celebrated while we are alive. But you know it doesn't happen that often. Maybe there should more of these celebrations of life when we are alive. However after many years of being a Funeral Celebrant, I sometimes get the impression that the funeral I have just conducted was the first and best celebration of that person's life.

There is the age-old truth that tomorrow is promised to no-one and that most people will only get one funeral. There has been the occasional exception to this rule. Some people have been pronounced dead and a service has taken place for that person, only for that person to re-appear some time later. But we all know, most people only get one funeral, unlike a wedding of which you can have several in life. The average couple probably spend months preparing for their wedding but, if you are lucky, your family will get four or five days to prepare for your funeral when you die (that is the average time in Scotland, in England it is slightly longer).

If you take charge of your own legacy now and write your own obituary/eulogy, you can almost guarantee that you will be remembered in a way that you are happy about. When you take the time to write your own eulogy, not only does it becomes your personal life story but it is one of the last and kindest acts you can do for your family and friends. As much as your family may love you, when you die, recalling the best and most significant details of your life is an overwhelming responsibility. Don't get me wrong, most families do a great job and people are probably spoken about in higher terms by their family when you are gone than when you were alive. They may well paint a better picture of you than you might paint of yourself. But the family will really appreciate it, when that day comes, if you have something already written down on paper, some basic points on how you would like to be remembered. It is a sobering point that when you are gone and have left this mortal coil, all your knowledge is gone too and it can never be recovered. Having a eulogy/obituary already written in advance overcomes this problem to some extent.

What do you believe your legacy to be? How would you measure your success on this earth? What do you think the story of your life will be like when told from the perspective of others? What would you want people to say about you when you die?

I recently took this one step further and wrote my own mother's funeral eulogy then I also decided that I would write my own (see Chapter 10).

Although, a word of caution about interviewing people from your own family and writing up their funeral eulogy. You can unearth all kinds of new information, some of which you might not want to know.

A fellow Celebrant interviewed her own mother and was startled to find out that she had three husbands! No one in the family knew except a sister and a brother and some close friends because most of them had either died or moved away. This information was not something the daughter had expected to uncover as she interviewed her mother in her final months on this earth. In her earliest years, before she had children, the mother in question had married a very successful banker who sadly died of a heart attack at the age of 32. That was followed by a second marriage that only lasted six weeks because he worked in the circus and literally left town one day and never came back. This was all unknown to Joanne, the daughter. All she had known was that her mum married a quiet man called Albert, who ran a family funeral business. Once she got over the shock of this news, she asked her mum all about her previous lovers. She was curious about exactly why she fell in love with each of them. Her mum said, 'Well I married one for the money, two for the show and three to get ready and go go go'.

I'll come clean, that story comes courtesy of a newsletter from the Australian Association of Civil Celebrants. But it had you going and reminds us about what can be uncovered when you interview people in advance and the importance of writing some kind of eulogy or legacy statement down.

The same caution should be applied to finding the right speaker. We have to be so careful about who speaks at a funeral. Over the years I have asked many people about their funeral experiences. Almost everyone I ask can tell me of some horrendous funeral they have experienced.

You don't get a second chance. If the Minister or Priest gets Aunty Mary's name wrong, if the officiant is a poor orator and has no stage presence – please feel free to go somewhere else. You are in charge. You are entitled to nominate the person you want to lead your service.

Chapter 9

My Way – Frank Sinatra

Conclusion.

'And now the end is near and so I face the final curtain'. The words from the famous song still rank in the Top 10 songs played at a funeral. I have offered a few more song suggestions within the book but there are hundreds of choices out there when it comes to choosing music for a funeral. That is what Civil Funerals are all about – choices and giving people the right funeral.

In this book I have highlighted the fact that the nature of funerals ceremonies in countries like Scotland is changing because families themselves want personalised funeral services. They want ceremonies that nourish and feed them and speak to them at the right level. Call them 'Celebrations of Life'; call them 'Civil Funerals' call them 'Bespoke Funeral Ceremonies', the title is not as important as the content and the delivery.

As Dally Messenger III, the founding father of the Celebrancy movement said in the foreword 'Words have great power' to move people. Words within a funeral ceremony have even greater significance because they are delivered at a one-off event that cannot be repeated. I have a deep conviction that funeral words must be delivered with the utmost passion, warmth, sincerity and conviction.

A family is saying their final farewells to someone they love and they have charged me with the last public words to be said in their honour.

Since the beginning of time it has been a noble act to bury the dead and pay tribute to them. What is even clearer now is that the right words must be said and they must be delivered effectively in order to allow families to grieve, mourn and be healed.

This book has argued that there is a new generation of people who are rejecting the 'one size fits all' approach to funeral ceremonies and are creating their own individualised ceremonies with PowerPoint slide shows, music and readings that appeal to them. These changes demand a new kind of person to lead the ceremony, someone who will walk with bereaved families along the path they need to walk. Civil Funerals accept the fact that families know best and Civil Celebrants feel honoured to be part of their final farewell. Civil Celebrants represent no-one interests except the family's. We speak for the family as an advocate, for those who would like to speak on a funeral day but feel they can't.

That is why this book focused on the art of public speaking at a funeral and offers itself as a guide to those already within the profession and those seeking to join it. It is vital for Celebrants to have great speaking skills because a funeral is a speaking event like no other; we speak for those who cannot speak because of sorrow and grief. Celebrants must study and practice the art of storytelling and continually develop the basic speaking skills such as pause and punctuation. Celebrants should accept the joy of knowing their voice is an instrument and that they are an artist.

This book aims to help Celebrants fine tune their speaking skills so that a life will be captured and painted in a way that will heal a family. The book highlighted many stories and examples where the Celebrant can be caught off-guard and that is why it focussed on three practical steps of; breathing, voice variation and body language. These areas must be mastered particularly for the more challenging funerals for babies and children, murder and suicide.

The right words can help families move forward with their lives. As Pam Vetter says, "A funeral is a speaking engagement and a Celebrant's work includes how to capture a life story in a moving way. I do believe a Celebrant is an artist as public exposition is not for everyone. If everyone could do this work easily, families would all be conducting their own family services. While there are a few family members who willingly share brief eulogies, there are few who want to conduct a full service when they are grieving. Therefore, the importance of a Celebrant being at his or her best is critical to the future of the entire movement. For a Celebrant, it's oftentimes a balancing act acknowledging that someone has died yet focusing on how someone lived life. But it's all in the delivery. When it's done right and with balance, we can feel the love for the life lived."

Aspire to inspire for those who have expired. Know the privilege of being invited into people's hearts and homes and above all respect their wishes, beliefs and values.

It's all about choice. Your gran may tell you one day that she wants her coffin to enter the crematorium to Abba's 'Dancing Queen' because that was her 'signature' song, the one she sang at the family Christmas party. A family may request Peter Kaye's 'Road to Amarillo' for their amusement, they can have it. It could be worse. They could have requested Monty Python's 'Lumberjack Song' as the congregation left and the next track is accidentally left on and as people leave the crematorium they hear, "Good evening ladies and gentleman... isn't it awful nice to have a penis", blasted out of the speakers (that genuinely happened by the way at Kirkcaldy Crematorium).

If the wrong song should be played in error the family still need to feel secure in the knowledge that the Celebrant will hit the right note with the words that will be delivered. It is all about trust, reducing stress on the day and healing the family so that they can move on from their real loss.

Trust and choice. That is why I offer a choice in the following chapter with two versions of my own eulogy.

Chapter 10

My Life Flows On – Aled Jones

How to write your own eulogy –
I offer you my own life story for my funeral.

Version one

My dear friends can I please on behalf of Neil's family thank you for being here today. He would like it to be said, that he would be overcome with sheer indifference that you have come along here today.

In case anyone is wondering why there are glass panels on the side of his coffin, it is just because Neil wanted to see who has not come along today.

Last week, whilst sipping a Jack Daniel's at his family home on Lake Lucerne in Switzerland, Neil passed away. He died peacefully in the arms of his beautiful wife of fifteen years, the former model and runner up in Miss Auchtermuchty (1984). He would like to publically acknowledge the joys of diamorphine and would like to ask for greater sympathy for all recreational users of the drug.

As you all know from the announcement in OK magazine and The Beano, Neil's ashes are to be blasted into space next Wednesday 5th November at the play park next to his house and souvenir hats, scarves, badges and cd's will be available on the day. There will also be a live broadcast on You Tube and we will play the 90 minute pre recorded message that Neil wishes to give to his family, his friends and the tax man. Amongst other things, he will highlight the couple of times when a smile did appear on his face, these apparently being the time his wife showed him her new silicone implants and Dundee United's memorable Champions League victory against Barcelona in 2028.

And it is with a smile and, of course, a heavy heart that I welcome you all here today. I especially welcome those who have travelled great distances and from distant galaxies to be here. There are apologies from Ronald MacDonald, and Forest Gump and a message has also been received this week from George Bush who was sorry to hear that Neil is deceasified.

But please don't be sad today. Neil's death was like his life – short and sweet. Looking on the bright side, he has left a wonderful legacy of 18 children, 32 grand children and 7 great grand children to help run his successful funeral business 'Living In A Box'.

Neil, as many people will know from his auto-biography 'The Idiots Guide to be an Ephologist' (now available at Bargain Books priced 99p), led a colourful life as; a rag and bone man, a film star, a double glazing salesman, a Funeral Celebrant and an Ephologist. I am sure that if Neil was here right now he would say that the last 30 years of his 46 years, when he did eph-all, were amongst the happiest of his life. It is funny how Elton John says; there is a circle of life because the first few years of Neil's life and the joys of lactating strangely resembled his last few years.

Neil, as you all know, was born in Dundee as a baby and did all the usual things of life. He grew up into a boy, then a teenager before he progressed into being a small man. But like poison we know that good things come in small packages. "Stretch" as he was affectionately known to many of his friends at school was always a popular and good looking boy. He was extremely bright, deliciously handsome, danced like John Travolta and ate lots of humble pie.

We are in no way attempting to polish the rim of Neil's halo here, there were moments in his life when he could be awkward and cantankerous and on many occasions he disproved Mr John's theory of life being circular by being a complete square.

Although to be fair to Neil, you don't have 10 wives and 18 children without demonstrating some degree of sex appeal and the DVD that Neil produced on this very subject is still one of the all time best sellers on Bid Up TV.

For Neil life was very simple: breast is best, don't eat yellow snow, no matter how much you may like your fellow man and woman some people are just ass h*!&*' and as you get older the more important people in your life are taken too soon and the ones you don't like, never go away.

Clearly that last message applies to no-one here, Neil really did have a lot of time for all of his friends and that is why the decision was made to keep the number of people at this funeral to single figures.

Over the years, in addition to his regular jobs as a professional speaker, rap artist and translator of Dundonian,

Neil spent several years working with young people in youth clubs and was well known for reporting them to the Police for Anti Social Behaviour Orders and throwing empty Budweiser bottles at any teenagers who wore baggy pants that exposed their Primark underwear.

Neil was a great believer in the after life and was always conscious of the fact you have to live in eternity with the clothes you are buried in. He has therefore fulfilled his final wish and is being buried today in a Santa outfit. He wishes however to dispute the scurrilous accusation from all his former wives that they only got one visit a year whereupon Neil proceeded to empty his sack.

Neil will be remembered for something one day, in the meantime he asks you to support his children with a collection at the end of the service for their college bursaries.

His final words as he saw the light coming towards him were 'Forward with Dorward.'

Version two

There are possibly many words that can be used to describe Neil; loyal, a man of integrity, sincere, a man of substance, quiet at times, witty, reliable, hard working and kind of cute. He was a son, a brother, a friend, a daddy and a husband.

But words are…well they are only words aren't they? Just ink blots on paper. Words only make sense when they are connected to an experience and a heart and what we are doing today is thanking Neil for being part of our lives and making our lives that bit richer and better just by being in them.

Most people's experience of Neil is that he was a thoroughly decent man and that he had a certain gift for bringing words to life within his work as a speaker and Funeral Celebrant. Not a great writer or speller; just ask his brother Philip how many hours he put in to editing his first book. But he was a great believer in writing your own eulogy and these are the words that Neil has left us.

He said he had a happy childhood, would spend hours upon hours playing football. He was a great Dundee United fan as a teenager and saw The Terrors in their prime of the 1980s. During his teenage years he joined a youth organisation called the Air Training Corps, 2449 Carnoustie Squadron and absolutely loved it. This was the making of the real Neil Dorward. By the time he was 15, he was up there at the front of a classroom, with his acetates for the overhead projector to teach fellow cadets about aerodynamics and the principles of flight. It was something he prized, being up there; training, sharing his knowledge and learning, trying to enthuse an audience on whatever it was he was speaking about.

He was a great believer in on-going development and spent nine years in university education and studied to Masters Level. When he put his mind to it he was dedicated to learning and improving himself and would gladly share that knowledge with others. He just quietly went about doing what he had to do without making too much of a fuss. His love was gentle, consistent and on the level.

Neil had a gift to communicate to people on their level and was a successful and popular Civil Funeral Celebrant, trainer and professional public speaker. The world of Civil Celebrancy in Scotland would not be where it is today had it not been for Neil. He trained numerous Celebrants and brought the internationally recognised Diploma in Funeral Celebrancy from Australia to the UK.

For a considerable period of his life Neil enjoyed offering his own time to helping young people. Neil, along with many amazing helpers, ran youth clubs in Dundee and Kinross for 11 years and took young people all over the world to amazing events like the World Youth Day and the Nolly Barge in Glasgow. He was an organiser. If Neil said he was going to do something he did it. If the local community council in Kinross needed a new mini bus Neil lobbied for it, if young people needed a £33,000 subsidy to take them away to Rome for 12 days he did it.

Neil said in his heart of hearts the one day if he felt that desire to be married, he would do it. Ok, it maybe took him five years or so but he made the decision and the 17th December 2003, the day he solemnly married Clare Bonucchi was one of the happiest days of his life closely followed by the birth of his beautiful daughter Katie Marie on 14th April 2005 and being a step dad to Roisin and Larissa.

Neil was always a bit of an amateur philosopher, a thinker; he liked to have time for himself and his own thoughts. For many years that bloody lap top of his was glued to his hand. But he was no bother to anyone and on the whole Neil was fairly easy to live with once you got used to his occasional moods and his tendency to avoid doing any DIY and gardening. Thank God he married a very practical woman who treated him with the utmost respect and kindness. They might not have lived in each other's pockets but they had a great marriage and he felt blessed to be loved by a very good wife and mum.

Neil conducted hundreds of funerals in his life, spoke at major events and felt very lucky in his life. He never asked for that much really, ok he pestered Clare to buy him a second hand Audi TT, which he got and posed about in but he just doddled through life and tried to be the best husband and daddy he could be. He knew he was deeply loved by his family and he had a very contented life. He believed that death was not the end, that true love never dies and ask us all to hold on to that faith today.

His final request was that his eulogy did not go on and on. 'It will be like me', he said, 'short and sweet'.

About the author

    Neil is one of the most experienced Civil Funeral Celebrants in the UK. He is a member of the Professional Speakers Association, the joint President of the Association of Independent Celebrants and the Director of Studies for the UK Division of the International College of Celebrancy. He divides his time between speaking at funerals, coaching, training people to become Civil Funeral Celebrants and delivering keynotes and workshops on the theme of 'Legacy' and 'This is your life'.

CPSIA information can be obtained at www.ICGtesting.com
Printed in the USA
BVOW07s1949191213

339630BV00001B/99/P